EASY NEWBORN
CARE TIPS

*Proven Parenting Tips For Your
Newborn's Development, Sleep Solution
And Complete Feeding Guide*

Author:

Lisa Marshall

Aknowledgement

I would like to thank my family for the extraordinary support in this process of research, writing and publishing of this book.

I would love to thank Dr Lisa Bates, for her wonderful collaboration. She supported me greatly and were always willing to help me.

I would like to thank Emanuela Antonelli, an expert in communication, for her support.

I would like to thank all the University Professors, Doctors and Experts mentioned in this book for their expert advice and encouragement throughout this project.

Finally, I would love to thank all those parents that I interviewed and who helped me, this book would have been impossible without them.

Thank you for purchasing this book. Click on this link to download this free tool

https://bit.ly/2FAGaqX

Note: If you have purchased the paperback format then you need to write this link on your browser search bar. This tool is a useful resource to understand the development of the language and communication of children. It is also a checklist on language and listening skills that will provide you with effective tips. All in all, it is a fundamental tool that will help you become an expert on parenting!!

"The moment a child is born, the mother is also born. She never existed before. The woman existed, but the mother, never. A mother is something absolutely new."

(Osho)

My name is Lisa Marshall, I'm an author expert in parenting and communication psychology, I assist parents, teachers and special educators, but first of all, I'm a mom of two beautiful children, Leo and Sonia. Thanks to them I start this research which led me to work with many experts that increase my knowledge of children's universe.

I wrote this book with the intention of providing tips and comprehensive answers to many questions that often arise to first time parents, providing them with proven and effective skills that can be used in typical situations that occur during the first months of a child's life.

It is important to understand newborn behavior, to know his needs and being able to interpret non-verbal language that the newborn uses to express himself, such as body language, crying and other small subtleties that you will learn to notice thanks to the informations I will give you in this book.

If you want to learn more about children you can find other books in my **Positive Parenting** series.

I wish you a good read.

Table of Contents

Introduction

Congratulations on downloading *Easy Newborn Care Tips* and thank you for doing so.

There are plenty of books on this subject on the market, thanks again for choosing this one! Every effort was made to ensure it is full of as much useful information as possible, please enjoy!

The attention and care parents provide to their babies helps them to develop and keeps the baby safe.

The feeling of having a child is beautiful and unique. But it is crucial to know that babies need special care and that care begins right from the moment of their birth.

From the very first day, attention must be paid to dealing with the baby, even to create a bond with both the mother and the father, since this is essential for the development of the child. For you to be prepared with the arrival of your little one, we've crafted this fantastic book that helps you cover up all the essential steps to parenthood and what you need to do to raise your baby well.

While there's a lot that you need to cover up, let's take a look at the five most crucial steps every parent MUST be aware of.

Availability

Your baby needs to be cared for all the time. Care in the beginning, in general, refers to the physical needs of the baby, which include changing diapers, bathing, and breastfeeding, being wrapped and picked up. Also, your baby lives a total dependency on another being to survive, and ideally, the one who can provide this care is the mother. Your baby needs to feel the real presence of his or her mother, as often as possible. In biological children, the attachment of the baby and the mother develop when the baby is in the womb, and the baby will recognize the mother instantly. In adopted newborns, the parents must form and strengthen this bond with their babies. While it's not as easy as it is with biological children, it's possible when you stay available for your baby when they need you.

Routine

For the baby to develop well, it is necessary to have a regular care routine, and the caregiver is the same person, preferably the mother. One day must be equal to the other so that your baby can feel safe. Routine and predictability of care significantly contribute to the baby's ability to organize and develop psychically. This routine not only makes it easy for your baby to feel safe, but it also makes it easier for the parents to get stuff done regularly without any surprises.

Sleep

A newborn needs many hours of sleep, which could be anywhere between 15 to

18 hours a day. However, your baby will need to wake up to feed every 2 - 3 hours. The range varies from baby to baby. Some little ones, from birth, sleep through the night, but in most cases, this does not happen. Therefore, it is vital for the mother or father to rest while the baby is asleep so that they are available to take care of the baby when awake. It's not comfortable to sleep for brief intervals so a breast pump can work wonders because the mother can keep bottles handy for the father when it's his turn to hustle with the baby at night.

It is also essential that, from the beginning of the baby's life, a sleep routine is established, so that the baby gets used to it and develops good sleeping habits. Differentiating the day from the night can help your baby to sleep less by day, so it is crucial that you keep the clarity and noises of the house while your baby sleeps during the day, maintain silence and reducing the brightness to the night, as well , so your baby learns to differentiate the day from the night. Over time, this insight helps your baby to sleep more at night.

However, if the baby wakes up, even at dawn, it is important that he or she be attended to. Your baby will wake with any of the following needs, which are usually hunger, pain, or a diaper change. And it's up to the parents to figure out what it is and be available to them, so they grow up to be strong, secure and independent children. Keep reminding yourself that infancy isn't going to last forever and no matter how daunting these tasks seem right now, it's something you will miss most about being a parent.

Holding Your Baby In A Secured Manner

When your baby was in the mother's womb, your baby was wrapped around the walls of her uterus in an aquatic environment, where he or she sensed the balance of his mother's movements, which gave your baby a feeling of warmth. After birth, your baby began to live on a still and rigid surface, which is very different from the maternal womb your baby was accustomed to. Therefore, you need to facilitate the adaptation of this little being and provide a warm cuddle whenever required. A swaddle also works wonders to keep your baby secure while asleep.

It is always the parents who provide security to a newborn. When holding your baby, you need to give him or her as much security and tranquility as possible, so that your baby feels balanced and "safe." The basis of personality will be well-established firmly when your baby is adequately secured. When holding your baby, make sure you have a firm grip over the head, and your other hand is wrapped around your baby's body.

Touching

Touching is critical to the baby's physical and psychic development and is essential for his or her adaptation to the world. Whether it's changing your baby's diapers, bathing, or even a massage routine, the loving touch at any age of the baby contributes significantly to your physical, psychic, and motor development. Some studies show that babies who had their bodies touched and massaged benefited with weight gain, among other benefits related to psychomotor development.

In the early months, it is convenient to leave the baby wrapped in the crib in a blanket with rollers or cushions around them so that he or she can touch them when while moving. This is an excellent way for your baby to feel welcomed, nested, facilitating the adaptation into the world in which you, as new parents have welcomed your bundle of joy!

Now that you've got your basics covered, let's take a closer look at what you need to do to be a hands-on parent to a newborn.

Chapter 1:
Understanding Your
Newborn Child's Behavior

Understanding the needs of your child always takes time so you need to be patient once you become a parent. Parenting is a journey and there are going to be hiccups along the way. All you need to do is stay prepared for them and face them together so you can raise a baby that's healthy and happy. You need to remember that all babies are different and while something may have worked really well for one child, it doesn't necessarily mean it will work for your own. You know your baby the best and you will eventually figure out what your child likes and dislikes and what works well for your child. Always speak to a doctor irrespective of what other people tell you. When it comes to taking advice, listen to everybody but do what your heart tells you to do and do not ignore suggestions made from a doctor or a medical representative. The transition from breastfeeding to feeding your baby solid foods is always going to be challenging but as long as you face it with confidence and you give your baby time to adapt, you will manage to feed your baby healthy meals right from infancy till they grow up.

Colic

Although the percentage is very small, babies do develop Colic. Colic is nothing but spells of crying that will last for hours on end. Some babies even end up crying for the entire day or the entire night. There is no medication that is available for colic babies and you need to make sure that you find ways to soothe a baby when this occurs.

How To Prevent Colic While Breastfeeding?

Colic is the condition that causes severe pain in the abdomen of a child and it is usually caused by the kind of food that you eat. Food such as cow's milk, cauliflower, broccoli and spicy food as well as chocolate can cause colic in a baby. Make sure your baby is healthy and does not suffer from these problems, by avoiding all of these items.

Colic has been a mystery for so many doctors and there are a number of theories related to colic. Colic usually applies to any child that is continuously crying for more than 3 to 4 hours on a daily basis. If this happens for one or two days then that is absolutely fine however if it continues for three or more days in a particular week then that is a cause for concern. Some children continue crying for more than 3 days a week and this goes on for more than 3 weeks. If you had a full-term baby then colic will usually begin when your baby is around 2 weeks old. If your baby is premature then colic will start later than two weeks. Doctors usually say that colic goes away by the time the baby is 3 or 4 months old. Contrary to belief, the sex of the baby, as well as the feeding habits, does not really affect colic. There is really no difference between people that had colic when they were babies versus people that didn't have colic. Here are a few theories with regards to what may cause colic and how you can help your baby calm down:

- Gas problems

- Hormonal changes that usually result in your baby being in a fussy mood

- The muscles in the digestive system paining due to the growth of the digestive system

- Nervous system of your baby slowly developing

Some parents even misunderstand certain conditions like colic and they usually panic. If you are really concerned then make sure that you take your baby to a doctor and find out the reason why he or she may be crying a lot.

Here are a few reasons why your child may be quite irritable and tend to cry a lot:

- An infection that may make your child feel uncomfortable

- Any kind of inflammation in the nervous system or the brain

- A child suffering from irregular heartbeats

- Any minor injury to the muscles or maybe to any of the bones

- Any kind of eye problems that the child may face

Treating Colic

Your doctor will be able to prescribe the ideal treatment for colic based on the tests that are done for your child. Ideally, there are things that need to be done one step at a time and you will need to see if your child calms down before you try the next step. Before you try too many remedies you should know that colic will get better on its own and you will need to be patient with your baby's development. Here are a few things that you could consider doing in order to ease the discomfort for your baby:

Feeding Habits

Although the feeding habits of the baby are not directly related to colic they can cause a bit of irritation and you need to see if switching between breastfeeding and formula helps reduce the colic in your baby.

Swallowing Air

If your child is facing gas related problems then you could try getting a special bottle that will help him or her swallow less air. You also need to make sure that your child sits up while feeding so that less air goes into the mouth. Also, make it a habit to burp your child during the feeding session and even after the feeding session.

Soothing The Baby

You could try various ways of soothing your baby and calming them down. This could be done with motions such as walking or rocking your child and it could also be done with the help of sounds such as singing for your baby.

Body Language

During the nonverbal stage of a child's development, a child's only way of communicating is through their behavior and body language. Children are very honest and direct and are conveying messages to those around him or her indicating what they need at that time.

By taking the time to watch and listen you will be able to better read the messages that your child is sending you and better respond to and fulfill their needs which will create a happier more well-adjusted child with a greater level of self-esteem. This willingness to read and respond will act positively on the development of the child's personality and temperament. Taking the time to tune in to your child's gestures and nonverbal communication style is essential to they're healthy development.

0 - 3 Months

During the first few weeks of life, your newborn seems to send a wide variety of signals. After birth, he turns his head when you touche his cheek, and extends his arms and legs crying when he is frightened, even he takes a step forward when his feet touch a flat surface or grabs your finger when you caress his palm. Dr. Speer (Assistant Professor Pediatric Surgery at the University of Texas), states that "It is interesting to note that none of these body signals is true communication. These are simply reflexes with which your child was born."

In a few months, some will disappear completely, while others will evolve into more targeted actions. Of course, not all of your baby's first signs are mere reflexes. The smile that emerges at around 6 weeks, for example, is not false. Ron Marino, director of general pediatrics at the Winthrop-University Hospital in Mineola, New York, states that "Your child's smile is not always an answer to your actions, but it is a sign that he is happy ... The parents work hard during those first six weeks of the baby's life, and it's nice to have feedback. "

4 - 8 Months

At 4 months of age, your baby's physical signals are clear because he begins to learn the cause and effect and coordinate thought and action. It is and it will be him, from now on, to use signals to indicate his desires and his needs, for example raising his arms when he wants to be raised, or kicks his high chair when he is tired of sitting, or throwing a toy when he wants to play with you, because this is a clear invitation to play. Children of this age can also use body language to indicate that playful recreation is over. Signs such as turning himself back or interrupting eye contact usually mean that your child has received enough stimulation or simply wants to play with his toys alone. During this time, our child is able to confuse us with some gestures that do not seem even remotely related to cause and effect. He can, in fact, pull his ears or move his head back and forth to indicate he is tired.

9 - 12 Months

Around 9 months, most children experience an explosion of cognitive growth. Mobility and eye-hand coordination improve, gestures are more specific, clear and communicative. From now on he will be able to easily demonstrate his desires and needs, likes and dislikes. A baby can welcome a familiar face with outstretched hands or cling tightly to the mother or father when anxiety for a stranger begins to emerge.

For example, at 1 year of age, if he is hungry, he can hit the bread drawer in the kitchen, or when he is thirsty, he places himself in front of the refrigerator, but he can also begin to match his signals with a variety of sounds. In a short time, the child's body language will be replaced with simple words and sentences of three words, hoping that they are easy to decipher. That's all? One of the most interesting indicators is the ability to reach intimacy - or links with other human beings - that is directly linked to our first interactions and comfort levels with our parents, primary caregivers.

Mom, I know what you're thinking: "Am I wrong, am I doing something wrong?" Other important ways the baby communicates his needs and desires are shown below. Some may seem obvious, but remember, babies speak an ancient language while adults rely on verbal indicators. Let us then review some linguistic manifestations of the body of our baby.

Baby Whining

What should a parent do? Our first communications with people around us are all non-verbal. Have you ever heard a three-day baby ask for a diaper change? No, babies in the first year mostly communicate through body language. And because it can be a source of confusion especially when deprived of sleep - babies cry, contort themselves and make confusion, trying to get proper attention and response, we often misinterpret what they are trying to say.

Getting a firm grasp on what the baby is trying to say allows us to raise that deep, ongoing bond between parent / caregiver and child. For some mothers this bond is immediate, for others it takes time, patience and a bit of work. By paying attention to the newborn's body language, you help facilitate this bond much more quickly - thereby developing the level of intimacy with your baby that needs to feel safe and loved. By understanding a lot of what babies are trying to communicate to us, we are aware that these movements are instinctual, they are the result of eons of evolution. Human beings are born with the ability to communicate - but not with the capabilities of spoken language. The language is artificial, a sub-product of the human condition, born from progress and necessity, not incorporated into our DNA.

For example, the "Moro reflex", common in newborns, is a phenomenon that disappears from the baby's repertoire at the age of four months when they adapt to life outside the womb. When this reflex is solicited, the baby grabs the air with the palms up and the thumbs flexed out and often the legs are similarly positioned. When we see these positions / movements, the child is reacting to fear. This reflex, which usually disappears after 3 or 4 months, is often a response to a sudden loss of support, often when a newborn feels like he is falling. It is normal, but the alarm-wake reflex can be avoided when he's going to sleep.

Head Rolling

The baby turns his head the other way when it is bored, disinterested or overstimulated. It's time to change gear! He rubs his eyes: often accompanied by one or two large yawns, it indicates fatigue. Studies have shown that the act of rubbing the eyes has a calming effect on the heart rate. He pulls and rubs the ears: when a part of our body touches another part, for example, rubbing the chin, screwing the hair, we want to indicate that we need comfort. In an attempt to console themselves, to get ready to sleep or to disengage from a particular situation, babies rub their ears to calm their emotions. It is easier to recognize these movements and gestures than to interpret their meaning. All babies are different, it is important to know and understand their behaviors and effectively establish their cause.

Arched Back

This is an act of rebellion, but when it is over-extended it can be a reaction to pain, almost always to heartburn, the most likely cause. If the newborn arches his back while feeding and crying or spitting excessively, it may be a sign of reflux or gastroesophageal reflux disease, a condition in which acid reflux from the stomach irritates the esophagus. If this behavior does not seem to be linked to nutrition, it can mean frustration and he asks for comfort.

Kicks Continuously

If he looks happy and smiling, this is probably a sign he wants to play, while if he is demanding or crying, it is an indication that something is probably worrying the baby. The cause can be anything from gas colic to a dirty diaper while sitting in a cramped car seat, but they can kick their legs simply because they can.

Head Banging

If you see your 10-month-old baby banging his head, like a wand, methodically on the hardwood floor or against the bars of his crib is an alarming attitude. But many babies do it regularly, and it seems that this does not cause any kind of pain, on the contrary: babies find the rhythmic movement forward and backward soothing. However, it should not be underestimated, up to 3 years, because if the child bangs his head for long periods of time, instead of engaging with others or playing with his toys, the pediatrician should be contacted.

Clenched Fists

Most newborns hold their hands in this resting position because they are not yet able to do much more, since the movement of the finger and hand requires a more developed nervous system and more complex brain function. Babies usually start to open their hands at 8 weeks and start reaching and grabbing for 3 or 4 months. Many times clenched fists can be a sign of stress or even hunger. If the baby's tendency to squeeze his fists persists after 3 months, it is good to have a pediatrician visit him.

Bent Knees (On The Abdomen)

This position is usually a sign of abdominal discomfort, or the presence of gas, a bowel movement, or constipation. It is important to try to alleviate the "ahi ahi!" If gas seems to be the problem, help him burp during feeding. If you breastfeed, check your guilty diet for producing gas from broccoli or potatoes. If you think constipation is a problem, it can usually occur when babies switch from breast milk to formula or when they start to taste solid foods around 6 months, check with your pediatrician for nutrition.

Self-Soothing

A number of parents witness their children banging their heads, rocking their body and rolling their heads from side to side during at times. While this may seem disturbing to you, be rest assured it is absolutely normal for your child to behave in this manner. The reason they do this is that it helps them to feel comforted and it is part of self-soothing. The common symptoms of self-soothing include:

- Staying in that position and rocking the body back and forth

- Sitting on the bed and banging the head towards the headboard

- Lying face down and banging the head and chest on the pillows or the mattress

- Moving the head from side to side while lying on the back

Making Noises While Rocking

Body rocking can start around 6 months while headbanging and head rolling is something that your child learns by the time they reach the age of 1. This behavior could continue between the age of 1 and 5 years but in some scenarios, children tend to continue the habit even post the age of 5.

Tips To Handle This Behavior

Keep a track of how long your child takes to fall asleep. If you notice that the time span is relatively long then this could cause headbanging in a child. Although a lot of parents want to go and try to control the behavior it is something that you need to stop yourself from doing. Children try to look at this as a method to grab attention and when you begin to notice or tell them to stop this habit will continue to grow.

The best thing to do is to protect your child and ensure that your child will not hurt themselves in any way. Try to get smooth rounded corners in all spaces of the bedroom and keep sharp edges away from your child.

When Do You Need To Seek Help?

While it is normal for a child to put themselves to sleep, if you notice that they do this throughout the night then this may be a concern and you may want to go check with your doctor. Some children tend to bang their head because of obstructive sleep apnea and it is important for you to treat this condition if you want them to stop.

Some children may suffer from intense conditions and this is why they bang their head and this could include developmental delays, spectrum disorder, autism or blindness. You will be able to differentiate between these habits and the normal headbanging habits if you notice that your child tends to rock the body and bang their head even during the day. While head banging and body rocking are normal when a child is trying to sleep, if your child is doing it even while they are awake then this is something you need to pay attention to.

Decoding Baby Crying

When the baby cries, he can have very different needs. We must not be taken immediately by anxiety and the fear that he is suffering, but concentrate on the characteristics of crying, listening to him, observing the baby's behavior to try to interpret his signal and respond appropriately. Here is a guide to help you evaluate the various nuances of the baby's crying.

I'm Hungry!

"Hunger cries usually begin as a low-intensity whine, then progressively increases to arrive, if the baby's need is not met, at the acute screams," explains Andrea Dotta, Director of the Neonatal Intensive Care Unit of the Bambino Gesù Pediatric Hospital in Rome. "It stops immediately when the baby is offered the breast, while the pacifier can only calm it for a few moments. To understand if a child is crying from hunger, of course, it is good to remember when he was fed last time, how long he sucked and if he sucked enough milk. "

Colic, Reflux And..

Immediately begins with shrill cries. "It's not a whine, but a scream," says the neonatologist. "In this way, the evening crying crises of babies suffering from colic or those of the little ones who have gastroesophageal reflux usually begin. Sometimes the crying of suffering can temporarily subside if the baby is offered the pacifier or, even better, the breast, because the movement of suction stimulates the release of endorphins and reduces pain. We must therefore be careful not to confuse it with the cry of hunger. The baby who suffers can suck for a while, but then it comes off and inevitably starts to cry again ". The most frequent causes in newborns are gaseous colic, gastroesophageal reflux and otitis.

"The baby is not able to describe his disorder, but parents can get some clues from his attitude and his movements. "If crying occurs with a certain regularity every day or almost, in the late afternoon or evening and the baby tends to contract the legs and flex them on the tummy, it is probably gaseous colic. There are no definitive remedies to eliminate the pain of colic, but usually babies who suffer from it benefit greatly from the tummy massages and from standing on their stomach, possibly in a belly-to-belly contact with their mother ".

The reflux tears occur instead during and after meals, because of the pain that the baby feels is due to the ascent of the gastric contents, which irritates the mucous membrane of the esophagus. "The baby breaks away from the breast frequently, bends his head back and arches his back," says the expert. Finally, otitis is more common in babies who are already a few months old than newborns. "Mom and Dad can recognize it by touching the baby's ears and watching his reaction," says Dotta. "In case of suspected reflux or otitis, it is necessary to consult the pediatrician for the diagnosis and appropriate treatment".

Discomfort

It is a less intensity lamentation than the cry of pain. "It is a sign that there is a discomfort factor in the environment where the child is: too much noise, too much light, too hot or cold, or a wet diaper," explains the expert. "Usually, the crying of the newborn has a plaintive cadence, without screams or sharp peaks, but it can grow in intensity if the cause of the problem is not removed."

Cuddles Time?

Does it make sense for a baby to talk about crying for a tantrum? "I would say no, at least not in the meaning that we attribute to this word for older children: sometimes, the little one cries because he wants to attract the attention of parents", Dotta replies. "He gets bored and wants to interact with adults and the environment, seeking the gratification of a mother's embrace and cuddles". Understanding the reason for the crying of a newborn is easy: to calm him, it is enough for the mother to take him in her arms, talk to him and keep him close to her. It is important to satisfy the need for physical contact of the newborn. For nine months, in maternal uterus, he experienced a condition of containment and, after birth, he needs to relive it in the embrace, in the skin-to-skin contact with the mother, in the rocking movement of her walk while cradling him, in the caresses. They are indispensable gestures to create the bond of attachment between mother and baby, and for the healthy, harmonious development of the future personality of the child.

Chapter 2:
Everything You
Need To Know About
Breastfeeding Your Child

Understanding Breastfeeding

Breastfeeding is something every woman should experience after childbirth not only because it helps to emotionally connect with the child but also because it has a lot of health benefits for the mother as well.

Breastfeeding Benefits For Mothers

Breastfeeding is healthy for women and there are a number of reasons why women should not shy away from providing their child with breast milk for at least 6 months. When a woman breastfeeds a child, it helps her to connect with her child, making her feel happy as a person. Women who breastfeed are less likely to suffer from postpartum depression and tend to be happier. They also look forward to nurturing the child and connecting with the child more effectively. This is because breastfeeding releases good hormones that help take out the physical and emotional drain that a woman she experiences during pregnancy. It releases two main hormones which include:

• Prolactin - This hormone helps to enhance the nurturing sensation in a woman and relaxes the child which focuses on the development during the early stages of infancy.

• Oxytocin - Helps build a strong bond between the mother and the child and makes a mother feel happy to hold the child close to her.

Women who breastfeed their baby post-childbirth manage to recover from pregnancy-related problems faster. Regular feeding helps to reduce the size of the uterus and bring it back to pre-pregnancy size a lot faster. It also helps to reduce postpartum bleeding which could drain a lot of energy out of a woman.

Women who breastfeed are less likely to suffer from ovarian cancer and they also manage to lose pregnancy weight more effectively in the process. It also helps women to reduce the risk of suffering from type 2 diabetes, cardiovascular disease, high blood pressure and high cholesterol and rheumatoid arthritis. Exclusive breastfeeding also acts as a contraceptive (Lactational Amenorrhea Method or LAM) because it helps to delay the menstrual cycle of a woman. This helps the body to cope with one pregnancy at a time and ensures that the second pregnancy does not occur too quickly. Breastfeeding caters to a motherly instinct in a woman that helps fulfill the urge to become a mother. It is also convenient because the mother doesn't have to worry about packing up too many things while traveling with a small baby. Breastfeeding is an affordable solution in comparison to formula that could cost you a lot of money.

Breastfeeding Benefits For Babies

There is no denying that breast milk is the best food for your baby and the advantages that this kind of milk offers are aplenty. Doctors all across the world encourage new mothers to breastfeed for as long as possible because it is natural and an integral part of the development of your baby. Even if you can breastfeed your child for as long as six months, it is something you definitely need to consider doing.

Breast milk contains a number of live ingredients which include healthy bacteria, stem cells, white blood cells, antibodies hormones and enzymes that work together to fight infections and prevent a number of diseases that occur in babies who are not breastfed. Babies who are breastfed are more likely to develop and grow healthier as compared to those who are not because they miss out on a lot of vital nutrients during the first stage of life. Breastfeeding decreases the chances of diarrhea or gastrointestinal infection as well. It is also less likely that a child who is breastfed suffers from an ear infection or chest infection from time to time.

The rate of sudden death infant syndrome in babies is higher when they are fed formula milk. Let's not forget the main reason why it is important to breastfeed your child. It is because it soothes a crying baby much like it provides comfort to someone who is hurt, and most parents underestimate how essential this is for the development of their baby.

Breastfeeding Premature Babies

Premature babies are more prone to conditions such as infections as well as fatal life-threatening diseases like chronic lung disease or sepsis. Nursing a premature baby with mother's milk can reduce the risks and can also increase the likelihood of the baby going home a lot sooner. Premature babies who are not provided with breast milk take a longer time to develop and become healthy in comparison to the babies who are nursed on a regular basis.

Help Babies Sleep Better

Breastfeeding enhances the sleep quality of a child and also enables a baby to go back to sleep faster as compared to when fed with formula. The more regular your baby's sleep and wake patterns are, the healthier your baby will grow and the faster you will notice development signs in a child.

Brain Development

The first six months are crucial in the development of a baby because this helps the growth of the brain increase at the speed that will never occur through the rest of the baby's life. If you want your baby's brain to develop in a healthy way, it is best to breastfeed. Children that feed through breastfeeding are more likely to achieve the desired milestones during the first six months in comparison to a baby that is fed formula milk. These children also tend to come out smarter and have higher IQs. The fatty acid present in milk is what enhances brain development and create a positive effect on the child. These fatty acids are only found in breast milk and cannot be replicated through any other formula.

It is also believed that babies that are breastfeeding do not suffer from behavioral issues as compared to children who are not. Children who are bottle-fed turn out to be more stubborn than the ones who were on breast milk for the first six months of their life. Even when you transcend to feed your baby healthy food, try to limit the use of the bottle as much as possible.

The benefits of breastfeeding are not just for the first six months of your baby but for a lifetime. Children develop a sense of security and attachment with their families and this helps them to deal with stress more effectively even when they grow up. Breastfed babies are less likely to suffer from various kinds of cancer such as lymphoma and leukemia. These babies also have better eyesight and stronger teeth. Breastfed babies are less likely to gain too much weight and become obese or suffer from diabetes. Let's not forget, breastfeeding is an economical way to nurture and nourish your baby in the healthiest possible manner.

Benefits Of Breastfeeding On Families

There is no denying that breastfeeding provides numerous benefits to the mother. It helps them develop a strong bond and keep them both healthy. Apart from being a great source of nutrition to the child, there are various other benefits of breast milk that can work well for the entire family.

No Expensive Equipment Or Formula Required

One of the major benefits of breastfeeding your baby is that you will be able to do so even in an economic environment without having to worry about spending too much money. Infant formula costs a lot of money and apart from investing in the formula; one also needs to take into consideration the tools and accessories required to prepare formula in a healthy manner. All of these items cost a lot of money and when a woman breastfeeds, she can eliminate these costs, making it easy for the family to cope with the additional member gradually.

Less Medical Expenses

There is no denying that babies who depend on formula fall ill more often and are prone to infection, including bottle infection that happens due to improper sterilization of the bottle or the other equipment used in the process. Children who are not breastfed also need to depend on various other medications to help them develop and this costs more money.

Emotional Stability

Babies who are not breastfed tend to get more insecure as they grow. Breastfeeding creates a natural bond between the mother and child and when this stage is eliminated, it becomes difficult for the child to adjust in a new environment. Babies who are not breastfed tend to get crankier as they grow and it becomes more difficult to handle them.

It Works As A Contraceptive

Research has shown that a woman who breastfeeds her child is less likely to get pregnant again in the first few months after childbirth (also known as Lactational Amenorrhea). This helps her body adjust to the new changes and still manages to keep her life normal with her family.

Time-Saving

A woman does not have to worry about the time that is required to prepare a meal for the babies because breast milk is always available. Infants are required to be fed multiple times a day and when a woman can breastfeed, it makes it easy for her to attend to the baby a lot faster and soothe the baby more effectively.

Less Stressful

A new mother is constantly worried about how she is going to look after her baby and when she has to think about an external factor of preparing formula, it puts more stress on her. Regular breastfeeding reduces the stress of having to worry about constantly being ready with food and always worrying about whether or not it will run out. It allows a woman to move around with her baby more confidently, knowing for a fact that she will be able to feed the hungry baby irrespective of where they are.

Tips For Your First Breastfeeding Experiences

The first 24 hours of a woman who is giving birth is more of what we could call a roller coaster ride. There's a lot of emotions and stress that women go through and it's also a crucial stage for her to begin the journey of breastfeeding her baby. There are a lot of questions in the mind of a woman when they first begin to breastfeed. Here is a complete guide that will help you understand exactly what you need to do to breastfeed your child during the first few days post-birth.

Start Early

The sooner you begin breastfeeding, the more comfortable you will get with the concept and the healthier it will be for your baby. You should start feeding your baby the minute you get to hold your baby for the first time. Ideally, you should nurse the baby for at least an hour once you give birth so that your baby gets used to you as soon as possible and you have no trouble in feeding the child. If you cannot feed your baby immediately after birth, you may want to consider purchasing a breast pump to assist you. If your breast doesn't naturally secrete enough milk, then the best thing for you to do would be to use a breast pump because this will considerably increase the amount of milk that is produced and it will help you to feed your baby conveniently.

Check For An Early Latch

A baby latches onto the mother almost instantly and it figures out a way to circle the nipple even when they are just a few hours old. If your baby has not latched on in the first few attempts, then you may have a latching issue. This is, however, a very rare scenario where babies do not manage to latch on to their mothers independently.

Babies Sleep Deep

Once the baby is born, they often fall into a deep sleep after a few hours and will not be able to latch as effectively as they could just after they were born. In certain cases, the baby latches on to you faster and they learn how to suck milk out of your breast and it makes the process of feeding the baby that much easier. Even if you haven't managed to get hold of a breast pump almost instantly and your baby wasn't able to drink milk soon after birth, there is no need for you to stress. You can always try and breastfeed a little later.

Breastfeeding - Days 1 To 3

Nurse Frequently

For the first few days post-delivery, you should keep your baby as close as possible because you will not be able to understand the exact feeding schedule of your child. When in the hospital, try to keep your baby skin to skin as much as possible so that you understand exactly when your baby is looking for the breast and you'll be able to feed your baby at the right time. Head bobbing, fist sucking and mouth fluttering are early signs of hunger, and this will let you know that you have to feed your baby.

No Artificial Nipples

You may not be able to nurse your baby very often but that doesn't mean that you should provide your baby with an artificial nipple or a pacifier to stay calm. A baby's stomach is small and all the milk that your baby needs is being produced by you. Avoid these pacifiers for as long as possible.

Colostrums Are Essential

For the first three days you lactate, your body produces a kind of milk known as colostrums. This milk is not a lot in quantity but it is the richest form of food your baby can get because it contains the necessary vitamins, proteins, antiviral agents and antibodies that help your baby get strong. This is the milk that works as a laxative for your baby and helps them poop.

Weight Loss

During the first three days of nursing, it is normal for your baby to lose about 7% of their weight. This is mainly because of the fact that they start pooping and the other fluids that were accumulated in their body start getting out of the system naturally. Most mothers believe that their baby is losing weight because they are not able to provide enough milk for the baby. The truth, however, is that your baby's stomach is the size of a marble and it eats no more than the amount that your body is producing. Switching to formula at an early stage may complicate matters for your baby and it may not work as well on your baby's digestive system.

Latching On Issues

If your baby hasn't latched on to you yet, there is no need for you to stress during the first few days; but if you are unable to nurse your child at all, then you may want to seek the advice of a doctor. There are going to be a lot of people who will come forward to give you unsolicited advice even though they have no medical background. The best thing for you to do is to avoid these and wait for the doctor and see what they have to say. You should also ensure you keep your baby skin to skin for as long as possible because some babies may find it a little difficult to latch on immediately but they may eventually. In the meanwhile, you should also extract the milk from your breast with the help of a pump and feed it to your baby with a dropper or a small spoon.

Breastfeeding - Days 3 To 5

Your body should get adjusted to breastfeeding during this time and it gets easier for you to understand the schedule of your baby.

Better Milk Flow

By the third to the fifth day, the amount of milk your body produces increases tremendously and you become more accustomed to feeding your baby. Children also learn how to suckle faster and they learn how to drink more milk. It is during this time that you will notice your breasts growing thicker and fuller and if you are using a pump, you will also manage to measure the amount of milk that your body produces.

Overfilling Is Normal

Some babies may not drink as much milk as others and it may be difficult for them to latch on as effectively as well. If your baby is not latching on, the best way to prevent overfilling is to use a breast pump. Some babies have a strong appetite and in this situation, you will not need to worry about your breast overfilling because they will constantly drain out the milk by drinking it at regular intervals.

Hand Expressing

Sometimes your breasts get so full of milk that it is difficult for your nipples to come out and this makes it very inconvenient for the baby to suckle. In such situations, you can use reverse pressure by using softening techniques to help the nipple enter the mouth of your child. Hand expressing is basically holding the nipple between two fingers and trying to drain out a little milk to help your baby.

Gently Massage

Sometimes your breasts become so full with milk that it becomes difficult for the milk to come out conveniently and in such situations, massages can work wonders. Using an ice pack in between the feeding session can help relieve the soreness in the breast and also helps with the flow of milk.

Check Diapers

As soon as you start breastfeeding your baby, you will notice that the color of your baby's poop changes from a greenish-brown color to a light mustard yellow. You will also notice the frequency of the diapers getting wet will increase.

Breastfeeding - Days 5 To 7

By the time you reach the fifth day of nursing your child, you would have gotten accustomed to the routine of your child as well as how long you need to breastfeed your baby. Babies do not like to drink a lot of milk at one time but they need you almost every 2 hours which means you will be breastfeeding your child at least 10 times in a span of 24 hours.

Understanding Your Baby's Hunger

Once the milk starts flowing effectively, you will notice an increase in the weight of your baby. You may want to try and increase the time frequencies in between feeding your child but the minute you notice the signs of hunger such as fist sucking or head bobbing, remember that these are signs that your baby wants milk.

Feeding Time Can Change

Some babies have a fixed schedule with regards to when they need to be nursed and when they need to be put down to sleep, while there are others who do not. Sometimes they decide they are hungry even after they have just got a stomach full of milk. This is normal and it just shows that your baby is also learning to adjust to a routine.

Continue Checking Diapers

A healthy infant will poop at least three to five times in a span of 24 hours. It is important that there is enough quantity of poop and it should be in yellowish in color and sometimes seedy in texture. The color of the poop can also vary depending on what you have eaten. While some babies poop immediately after every feed, there are others who like to consolidate their poop and let it go in one shot. Usually at least 5 to 6 wet diapers are considered normal.

Check Your Baby's Weight

It is important for you to check your baby's weight as often as possible with a digital weighing scale since this is most reliable. In taking the right weight of your baby, try to keep your baby on the weighing machine without any clothes each time.

Get Help If Needed

It takes about two weeks for babies to go back to their original birth weight but by the end of the first week, you will notice a slight change in the weight. If your baby hasn't gained any weight after a week, consider visiting a doctor.

Take Supplements

Women usually focus on a lot of prenatal supplements while they are expecting but they tend to forget taking care of themselves once the baby comes along. If you want your baby to stay healthy, you need to stay healthy as well because at the end of the day your baby gets their nutrients from you. Not all mothers may be required to take supplements but always ask your doctor if you need any.

Tenderness Should Subside

By the fifth to the seventh day, nothing should be uncomfortable for you and you will not experience any pain when your baby is suckling. If it continues paining, then you need to visit a doctor. When your baby first latches on, there will be some mild tenderness which should fade away almost instantly but if it continues for more than a few weeks, then there is a problem and a doctor should definitely be consulted.

Once you pass the first week of breastfeeding, it becomes comfortable for you to feed your child whenever the baby is hungry and you will also be able to figure out exactly what your baby needs and when. Your body becomes accustomed to breastfeeding and you learn the most comfortable position in which you can feed your baby most effectively. This is also the state you should learn to start snuggling with your baby and increase the emotional equation.

Answers To Common Questions About Breastfeeding

There are a number of questions that come to mind for a new mother when she begins breastfeeding. Here we will try to cover as many of them as possible so that you have answers to all your questions when you embark on your journey of nourishing and nurturing your baby.

When Will Milk Start To Form?

Most pregnant women worry about milk not accumulating in their breast during the first few days of their pregnancy. The truth is your body has already started to produce a thick milky substance called colostrums which begins to form before childbirth and will be available in your breast for at least three days post-birth. The milk in your body will start to form after about two or three days and the quantities will continue to increase as you feed your baby.

Does The Size Of The Breast Affect The Amount Of Milk?

It is common for women with smaller breasts to worry about whether or not they will be able to feed their baby and produce enough milk. However, you need to understand that the size of your breast has nothing to do with the amount of milk that your body can produce because this depends on the mammary glands. And as soon as your baby drinks milk, your body will start producing more milk.

Why Is My Baby Still Hungry After A Feed?

While this is rare, sometimes you may not be able to produce enough milk to feed your baby. If the milk supply in your body is low, you can always speak to a doctor or an expert to help increase the production of milk.

Is Breastfeeding Easy?

This is the toughest question to answer because while breastfeeding is the most natural thing to do, it's not the easiest thing for every woman to begin in the first place. The initial few days are a struggle and usually accompanied with a lot of discomfort and pain but once women get past this stage, they will manage to nurse their baby more effectively and without any discomfort.

I Can't Tell If My Baby Is Drinking?

Sometimes a baby immediately latches onto your nipple but may not suck the breast. Sometimes they circle without drinking milk at all and this often confuses you with regards to whether or not your baby has a full stomach. You may want to see whether your breast feels lighter after feeding and this will help you determine whether your baby drank milk or whether your baby was just seeking comfort.

Is My Body Producing Enough Milk?

If your baby seems to be satisfied after a feed and stays relaxed for about 2 or 3 hours post-feed, there is nothing that you should worry about. Post-feed, babies take a good nap and relax, and this is a sign of a full stomach. You will also notice the difference between your breast before and after nursing. With the change in your baby every week, it is also a great way to observe whether you are giving your baby enough food or not.

How To Increase The Milk Supply?

There are a number of reasons why there is less milk produced in your body and if you think that the only way to increase the production of milk includes feeding your baby more frequently, you should know that pumping your breast soon after your baby has been fed and eating a healthy diet and drinking fluids also help. You also need to make sure you get enough rest so that you give your body the time to produce milk.

Soothing The Breast?

It is common for women to experience soreness in the breast and pain during the first few attempts at breastfeeding. Using a breast pump to release the milk or even an ice pack can help you to handle the pain.

How To Cure Sore Nipples?

Sore nipples are common during breastfeeding which is why you need to ensure that you do your best to prevent this condition and treat it as soon as possible. The minute your nipple starts to feel a little sensitive after feeding, try to dry them instead of immediately covering it up with clothes. Do not wear tight-fitting bras or clothes that can stick to your nipple because this can irritate the skin and cause a lot of soreness. Rubbing your nipple with a little breast milk is also a great way to help heal them.

Nursing If My Nipples Are Bleeding?

A lot of women tend to stop breastfeeding when the nipple starts to bleed. Apart from this being uncomfortable, they also believe that it could cause harm to the baby. The truth is that a little blood in your milk will not harm your baby in any way as long as you are healthy and you do not have any contagious illness. While cracked nipples or bleeding nipples do not occur so often, it usually happens when a baby has not latched onto the breast properly.

What To Eat Or Drink While Breastfeeding?

The one thing you need to keep in mind during breastfeeding is that moderation is essential. Well balanced and wholesome diets are something that will help you to provide the night nutrition to your baby and keep you healthy as well. Try to stay away from food items that will make you feel bloated. Drink a lot of water and consume fresh fruits as much as possible.

Is Breast Pumping Healthy?

Breast pumping is extremely beneficial to women who are not able to nurse the child naturally or whose baby has had a problem latching on almost instantly. It also comes in handy when a woman needs to go back to work and cannot stay home for the full day to breastfeed her baby. As long as the breast milk is stored nicely, it can be used to feed a baby later.

How Long Should You Breastfeed?

Some women prefer breastfeeding for up to as long as four years but this isn't something you should do if your baby has started to eat healthy food. Breastfeeding your child for the first six months without the introduction of any other food is necessary. Post 6 months, you should try and introduce your baby to solid foods so that your child learns to become more independent.

Getting Accustomed To Breastfeeding

Once you get past the first few weeks of breastfeeding, it will all be about learning how to accustom yourself to techniques that work well for you. Different women learn to adjust to breastfeeding with different methods. So you need to see what you are most comfortable doing and how well your baby is adjusting to breastfeeding so that you can benefit from it the most.

There are some suggestions that are great for breastfeeding while there are others that should be avoided. If you are not too sure whether you have found the right position to breastfeed your baby, then here are some positions that may help you.

The Cross Cradle Hold

One of the best positions to nurse your child is the cross cradle position. For you to nurse your baby effectively in this position, you need to be in an upright sitting position on a chair or a sofa that has an armrest. Bring your baby to your front and cross your arms as if you are cradling your baby around the body. Make sure your baby is as close to you as possible before you begin nursing. Your arms should be across from one another which means your left arm should control your right breast while the right arm should support the left. In case you do not have a chair or a sofa with an armrest, you can always use pillows as support. It is important for you to gently guide your baby towards your breast without leaning over your child.

When breastfeeding, keep in mind that it is important for your baby to breathe so the more you try to push yourself on your baby, the more the chances of suffocation. In babies who have difficulty to latch on the breast, it becomes easier for them to use this method because you will be able to guide your baby's head with your hand. Children also feel secure in this position because they are wrapped around in their mother's arm. You can also use this position to feed your baby while sitting on a bed by simply crossing your legs for support.

The Cradle Hold

If you are not comfortable with the cross cradle position, you can try the cradle position which is very similar to cross cradle, except that you will not be crossing your arms from one another but rather using your elbow as support. Different women have different body structures so it becomes difficult for them to use a cross cradle without putting too much pressure on the baby. If you do not want to stretch your baby out, then keep a pillow on your lap and use the cradle position to begin nursing. In the cradle position, you can use your elbow as a guide to help take your baby's head towards the nipple. When nursing your baby in a cradle position, make sure that your baby is straight and not turned to the side because this could cause suffocation during nursing.

The Football Hold

When you have a natural childbirth, it becomes easier for you to begin breastfeeding since there are no stitches on your stomach and you heal faster. However, in the case of a c-section, women take longer to heal and they find it difficult to breastfeed with a baby on the lap. If you have had a C-section and you cannot use the cradle or the cross cradle position to feed your baby, you can try the football hold. This is convenient since it doesn't put any pressure on your stomach and you manage to feed your baby with the help of your elbow. All you need to do is hold your baby sideways and use the head of your baby as if you were holding a football and bring it towards your breast. You must always keep a pillow on the side so that you have enough support for your baby and you do not lose balance while holding your baby. This position also works well for premature babies who are very small.

Lying On The Side

Lying on the side is an easy way to feed your baby when you are tired or when your baby is on the bed. It's an easy way to feed even if you're have undergone C-section or you are not comfortable with holding your baby in your arms and nursing. This is also the safest way to feed your baby for the initial few months. All you need to do is lie to your side and use your elbow to support the baby's head. Using your other hand, guide your baby's head towards the nipple and begin feeding. This keeps you comfortable and relaxed and when some babies need to drink for a longer duration, you will manage to do this a lot more comfortably.

Feeding Twins

Ideally, you should always feed one baby at a time even if you've got twins. But sometimes you can't leave another child crying while you tend to one and if both your babies are hungry at the same time, then the only alternative you have is to use the football hold for both. Use a chair that has an armrest. In such situations, you have to hold both babies on either side and feed them together. This takes a lot of practice so make sure that you have somebody by your side while doing this. They will help you with getting comfortable and also taking one baby at a time from you post-feed so you are able to get up. When you feed twins together, you need to stay as calm and composed as you can because you have to handle two children and that is not an easy task.

Breastfeeding Positions To Avoid

When you breastfeed your child, you need to make sure that you are feeding your child with precision and comfort. When you bend over your child to breastfeed, you will only block the nasal passage of your baby and it will be difficult for your baby to breathe while suckling.

Some parents choose to keep the baby's body and head in different directions while feeding. This is not good because it could damage your baby's neck and also cause them to choke more easily. When you nurse your baby, make sure that you bring your baby very close to your breast so that they are comfortable and are able to drink as much milk as possible.

Breastfeeding In Public

Just because you are breastfeeding your baby doesn't mean you have to stay confined to the house. Women are independent and have every right to step out even when they are breastfeeding and they can breastfeed the baby when in public. There is nothing to be ashamed about because breastfeeding is normal and is natural; and when you breastfeed your baby, you are providing your baby with nourishment in the most healthy way.

Know Your Rights

Breastfeeding in public is legal and there is nothing wrong with it because it is a biological need for your baby and it's the right food. Most women choose to breastfeed exclusively for 6 months which means they cannot give the baby anything apart from breast milk. While some women are comfortable pumping milk with a breast pump, there are others who choose not to use a pump and nurse a baby naturally whenever necessary. All you need to know is you need to be comfortable doing it and confident irrespective of what the situation is.

Practice

Before you head out with your baby with a mindset that you will breastfeed in public, it is always recommended you practice a little at home in front of a mirror just so that you get a fair idea of what a person sees when he or she is in front of you. Most women usually worry about exposing too much skin while nursing which is why they feel pressure to get confined to the home or go to a corner and try to breastfeed. You need to understand that when you are nursing your baby, your baby will cover up most of your breast so there is nothing that will be visible. You can also use blankets or a shawl to try and cover up while nursing your baby but this is something you will have to practice at home because some children cannot stand a fabric touching their face and will start crying, while others, on the other hand, are not bothered as long as they are being fed.

Choose Clothes You Are Comfortable In

It is important for you to stay as comfortable as possible when you are nursing so that you are able to do it more effectively. Front opening clothes are always advisable because you don't have to worry about pulling your top over your breast to feed your child. You should also consider investing in loose T-shirts because these are easy and accommodating. You can also consider wearing a tank top along with a cardigan. If the tank top has a stretching neck, you will manage to pull out one breast and feed your baby whenever required.

These days, there are a number of wraps available in the market that you can simply wrap yourself around with while nursing and this keeps you comfortable through the process. However, you can only invest in these things like a wrap if your baby is comfortable with a piece of fabric over the face while nursing. The reason you should consider getting a wrap is that you will never need to worry about the embarrassment of nursing and you can walk around while nursing if you have to.

An Easy Access Bra

While some mothers choose to wear a tank top without a bra, there are others who may not be able to have the luxury to do so because of the size of their breasts. If you cannot leave home without a bra, try investing in a sports bra that grants you easy access to pull up and down whenever required without struggling to reach for the strap. If you don't like a sports bra, you can also consider getting nursing bras which are easier to use. Nursing bras are easy because they come with nursing pads that provide your breast with a lot of comfort once you have completed feeding your child. When you invest in nursing bras, try to get a lower cup because this just makes it more convenient for you. Even with your bra, make sure that you practice opening it up and closing it before you go out in public.

Pick Your Spot

When breastfeeding in public, the one thing you need to make sure of is you choose the right spot for breastfeeding. No matter where you are, make sure that you are comfortable and you have your back well-rested so you do not hang over your baby. If you want to breastfeed in public effectively, always choose your spot beforehand so that when the time comes, you know that it is available to you. If your baby is fine with a wrap then you don't have to worry about getting prepared to breastfeed when your baby is hungry. You can always turn towards the wall and feed the baby so you feel more confident while breastfeeding.

Turn Away To Latch

Babies take a while to latch and this is the most venerable times for a mother because there is a lot of skin exposed during the latching on. If you want to feel comfortable before the latching on then use a blanket to cover up your front completely or turn towards a corner or a wall where you give your baby enough time to latch. Repeat the same when you are feeding and your baby has to latch on.

Smile

When you breastfeed, you will attract a lot of attention, irrespective of what kind of attention it is. While some people will be appreciative of what you are doing, others may look at you in a shocked manner while some may look down upon you. No matter what kind of reaction you get from others, always smile back at them because it shows that you're confident of what you are doing because you are concerned for the wellbeing of your baby.

Breastfeeding & Independence

Babies usually manage to switch between the breast and a pacifier or a bottle the very same day you introduce them to it. If you try introducing your baby to a pacifier or a bottle at a young age, there may be confusion. But when you try doing this post 6 months, you will manage to switch between the two conveniently and you will be able to transition from breastfeeding to other methods of feeding your child. This comes handy if you have to resume work and you cannot be available all the time to breastfeed. Mothers often worry about whether or not their child will be able to use a bottle or a pacifier and whether it provides them with the kind of security that they feel when they suckle on their mother's breast.

If you are planning to stop breastfeeding your baby because you have to resume work, you may want to introduce your baby to a pacifier and a bottle at least a few weeks in advance so you are confident your child is comfortable using this method of feeding. Babies will take a little while to adjust to a nipple that is artificial in comparison to the breast because your body is a natural way of feeding your child and it is designed in a manner to make it convenient for your baby to drink milk. When your baby sucks a bottle for the first time, the milk comes out with no control. This is because of the change in pressure. If you notice that your baby cannot drink the milk too fast from the bottle and a lot of the milk trickles down his or her face, then try to keep the bottle tilted a little so that the milk does not push towards the opening of the nipple very fast.

While some infants enjoy switching from a bottle to the breast, there are others who do not like the idea so much and would much rather stick only to the bottle or the breast. If you notice that your child is more inclined towards any one of them, try to make sure that they get comfortable with just that one method. If your baby finds breastfeeding more convenient, then you may want to stop breastfeeding for a while so they get used to drinking milk out of a bottle and do not crave the breast so much. To stop breastfeeding completely and get your child dependent on bottled milk, you have to wait for at least 6 months. Natural breastfeeding to the age of 6 months is highly recommended because this is what your baby needs and it works well for the development of your child.

Some children simply like to suck the breast for comfort even if they are not hungry and if your baby has the habit of doing this, then you may want to consider investing in a pacifier. Pacifiers can help them get some sort of security especially while they sleep because it feels like they are suckling the nipple. This also works really well when you have to move back to work and you want your child to feel comforted even when you are not around.

If for some reason, you cannot nurse your baby and you have to give your baby the bottle in the first few weeks of infancy, then you need to consider getting an infant bottle. If your baby cannot use the bottle then you may want to try using a dropper or a syringe to slowly feed the milk to your child. There are different kinds of nipples and bottles available in the market so make sure that you choose one you think your baby will be comfortable using. Invest in different kinds of bottles and a pacifier to figure out which one your baby likes the best.

Getting Your Baby Used To Formula

A child who is used to breastfeeding will take a while to get used to the formula for one basic reason - formula doesn't taste as good as breast milk and they long the taste of breast milk. If your baby is not really getting used to formula, then you may want to try another source of baby food that your baby might get used to. Apple juice with water is a great source of nutrition even when your baby is a few months old. Take a small amount of apple juice and mix it with water and try feeding your baby this juice at regular intervals. Once you start introducing other such foods, you can slowly introduce formula and other milk products that can help your baby get proper nutrition.

Returning To Work

Returning to work post-delivery is one of the toughest things for women to do not only because she is emotional about leaving her baby alone but also because she is worried about the wellbeing of her child. Unlike the olden days where women had the luxury of sitting back and watching their children grow, these days women are more career-oriented and need to focus on a career along with raising a family. There's nothing wrong with going back to work post-delivery as long as you prepare yourself and your baby for what lies ahead. Having said that, once you choose that you want to get back to work, you have to start preparing yourself mentally to be able to leave your baby alone. You also need to prepare your baby and learn to teach your baby some sort of independence so your baby can stay happy even when you are not around.

Set A Date

You need to set a date you believe you want to resume work because this will help you plan more systematically. Ideally, a mother should be with her baby for at least 6 months after delivery so that she gives her baby exclusive time as well as nourishment in the form of breast milk for the first 6 months. If you have to resume work before 6 months and you still want to continue breastfeeding, then using a breast pump is your best bet. However, if you plan on doing it post 6 months then you need to give your baby enough time to cope with external foods.

Once you have decided when you want to get back to work, you need to start preparing yourself mentally and physically and prepare your baby to get used to being away from you for long periods. Setting a date gives you time to prepare and plan exactly what needs to be done before you start working.

Check Your Baby's Weight And Monitor Progress

A few months down the line, you will manage to figure out exactly how much weight your baby gains each week and what is the progress that is required for your baby to remain healthy. If your baby is dependent on breast milk alone, consider using a breast pump to pump milk out and freeze it to be used later during the day when you are not around. If you do not want to give your baby breast milk exclusively, then you can also consider using formula. Try using formula a few weeks before you resume work so you can check the progress of your baby's weight and see how well your baby is reacting to it.

Get Your Baby Used To A Pacifier And A Bottle

If you are away at work, the only way your baby can eat is with the help of a bottle. It's important you get your baby used to a bottle and also make sure that you know exactly what kind of food your baby prefers. Make sure to stock up on ample bottles and keep the meals prepared well in advance. Learn the best storage options for breast milk as well as formula. If there is someone around to prepare the formula then always try to get it prepared fresh rather than keeping it prepared in advance. Make sure all the bottles are sterilized and cleaned effectively. This is why more bottles come in handy because on days when you have to rush, you have a spare that was already cleaned.

Practice Staying Away

While you may mentally prepare yourself walking out the door and heading to work with a smile on your face, once you say goodbye to your baby, it's a lot easier said than done. Leaving your baby and going to work is the most emotionally draining experience that a woman will face and you need to practice doing that so you are confident on the actual day. Try calling your friends and ask them if they want to head out to the movies and ask somebody to supervise your baby while you go out. Take a trip to your office if needed and check out your workspace. Ask your boss if you could spend a few hours working before you resume completely. This will give you a clear idea of how well-focused you are at work and how you are dealing with the emotions of being away from your child.

Supervision

Leaving your baby and going away is one thing to deal with but having somebody else look after your child is also a scary thought. Discuss with your partner the various options that you have with regards to caring for the child when you are not around. If you have parents or family members who are ready to look after your child when you head out to work then it's the best thing to do because you know these people will not harm your child and you will feel safe for leaving your baby with them. In case there is nobody you're related to who can take care of the child, you will have to consider two options - dropping your baby at daycare or hiring a full-time nanny.

There are pros and cons to both these options and it truly depends on what you think will work well for your child and his/her age. If your child is less than a year old, then they need personal attention and a full-time nanny who will be able to provide that. However, if your kid is a little older than that, then socializing is important so daycare might be a better alternative.

Secure Your Baby

If you're hiring a full-time nanny, make sure you have the house proofed with a nanny cam so that you can keep an eye on your child even when you are at work. While this seems a little extreme, it is always better to watch what's going on than to imagine things in your head. If you have family members in the vicinity, always ask them to drop in and check on your baby every once in a while.

Get Your Child Used To It

Whether you plan on leaving your baby at home with a full-time nanny or whether you plan on dropping your child at a daycare, you have to make sure your child is comfortable with the idea as well. Children blend in really fast but it takes them an initial 1 to 2 days to get comfortable with the idea. The best thing to do if you are keeping a nanny is to invite the nanny to come to stay over in your presence. You can explain exactly what needs to be done during the course of the day and get the nanny used to your child's routine. Let your child get familiar with them and let the nanny and your child spend some quality time alone. This will help your nanny gain confidence in taking care of your child. If you plan on leaving your baby at daycare, start with a shorter time span and gradually increase them to the hours you will be leaving your child there.

Figure Out If You Are Truly Ready

Once you have done all of this, always sit back and question yourself with regard to your decision and whether you are comfortable moving ahead with your plan. Make a list of everything you want to do to keep your baby happy and get it all ticked off before you get back to work. If you believe that your child needs a little more time with you, do not hesitate to get an extension. There is no denying that a mother knows what's best for her child so if you feel you need more time, always give your child that extra time so that you help your child develop better.

Breast Pumps

If you haven't already tried using a breast pump, you may want to consider using it to pump milk out of your breast because this is one of the most convenient ways of making sure your baby gets fed even when you are not around. Whether you are planning on getting back to work or simply living a more independent life with your partner that is helping you raise your baby, pumping milk out of your breast and storing it is something you should consider doing.

Pumping Your Breast Milk

You do not need to wait for a long time before you start pumping. Some women begin breast pumping as early as a few hours into delivery because this ensures that your baby gets a healthy feed even with latching on issues and it also increases the production of milk in your body without letting any milk go to waste. If you pump milk regularly, you will never suffer from any kind of swelling or soreness in your breast because of too much milk accumulation.

There are various kinds of breast pumps available in the market so make sure you choose one that works well for you. Before you begin pumping your breast, clean your hands well and make sure that you use a sanitizer that has at least 60% alcohol so that it sterilizes the environment. Always use sterilized bottles and sterilize the pump too before you use it. If your breast has a lot of milk, it will automatically start pumping out. If you need a little assistant, always try to think about your baby and apply warm and moist clothes to your breast to ease the flow. A gentle massage can also assist. When pumping out breast milk, relax as much as possible and get as much milk out of your breast as you can so that you can store it for your baby.

Storage Of Breast Milk

It is very important to understand how to store breast milk, otherwise, all your pumping efforts will go to waste. You can keep breast milk at room temperature for up to 24 hours once you have pumped it, but if your baby is not going to consume the milk within that time, the best thing to do would be to keep it in a refrigerator. Refrigerated breast milk can stay fresh for up to 4 days of pumping. You can also choose to freeze it and take it out whenever you need it. You get breast milk storing bags that are made specifically to freeze human milk. Make sure to purchase plenty of these bags and seal them properly before keeping them in the fridge.

Always make sure to mark dates on the breast milk that you have kept in the freezer so you do not use any milk that is stored for over 4 days.

Freezing Breast Milk

Understand the procedure for freezing breast milk so you do not let any of the milk go to waste. When purchasing breast milk in storage bags, always try to look for smaller bags so that your baby is able to consume one pouch while feeding instead of having two thirds and then feeling full. When filling a bag with breast milk, always leave a little space at the top of the bag because each item tends to expand when it freezes and the last thing you want is for the bag to explode when frozen. Always seal the back carefully to ensure that no external elements enter the milk while in the freezer.

Thawing Breast Milk

Before you feed your baby breast milk that has been extracted by a pump, you need to bring it back to room temperature. When choosing a bag of milk that you want to get out of the freezer, always look for the one that is marked the oldest. If you tend to use a breast pump multiple times a day, always enter the time as well as the date when it was extracted so you get the oldest bag fast.

While you do not have to warm up the breast milk, you need to make sure it's not too cold because this could cause your baby to catch a cold. You can leave this milk outside for a few hours so that you can use it directly without having to worry about warming it up. Once you have taken out a bag of milk from the freezer, it is best not to freeze the milk again. Try to use it within 24 hours of being outside the freezer. If it is inside the fridge, leave it outside for 2 hours at room temperature.

The more you pump milk out of your breast, the better the production of milk and it also helps the baby to learn to be independent. This works really well if you have to leave your baby at daycare, with a nanny or even if you have to head out for a couple of hours without your baby.

Breast Versus Bottle

Most mothers who give birth choose to breastfeed the baby unless there is a medical reason or some important reason why they choose not to breastfeed. In my opinion, if you can breastfeed, it is something you should definitely do at least for the first 6 months because this is a great tool to assist in developing a sleep routine for a baby, and it helps your baby feel very secure which helps to incorporate independence. Although lots of parents believe that breastfeeding will lead to dependence, it is in fact the opposite; a child that is breastfed turns out to be more secure and independent. You don't have to breastfeed your baby all the time. You can always use a breast pump so that your partner can assist you with the feeding habits from time to time. The reason I recommend breast milk is because it is healthier than formula, and if you can nurse your baby, then there's no reason why you shouldn't. For all those mothers out there, I want you to know that not only does breastfeeding help your baby develop better, but it is also a great way to get into shape. If you've been contemplating whether or not to do it, I highly encourage you to do it.

Although a lot of mothers believe that it is extremely stressful to nurse a newborn because of their feeding habits, the truth is that it's not going to be that difficult once you come up with a plan. So all you need to do is think about your child's needs, and then you will be good to go. Breastfed babies actually tend to sleep a lot better in comparison to formula-fed babies because of the security and the comfort they get during the process of breastfeeding.

Feeding at Night

For the first 6 weeks, your doctor is going to recommend that you feed your baby many times a day; this means every other hour, even at night. While you may feel that overfeeding your baby is wrong, this food is healthy for your baby and important for their development.

Babies tend to start crying and mimicking the sucking action when they are hungry. As I said, the first few weeks are going to be erratic, and it is going to be difficult for you to understand your baby's routine because your baby is trying to adapt to their new environment all of a sudden. The reason it is important for you to nurse every two hours is because this helps to increase your milk supply; once you have a substantial amount of milk forming in your breast, not only will you be able to use a breast pump more conveniently, but you will also be able to come up with a feeding routine without worrying about whether or not you will be able to nurse your baby.

A lot of mothers believe that just because the baby is awake at night, it means that the baby is hungry; however, that's not always true. Sometimes children just want to play around at night, so make sure that you check what's up with your kid before trying to feed them.

6 Weeks to 4 Months

After the initial 6 weeks, things get a lot easier, and you will start to recognize a routine with your baby. This is when you should decide what kind of feeding habit you would like your baby to adopt. By the sixth week, the number of times to feed a baby at night will reduce, and your baby will be able to sleep more effectively and for longer durations. This is when your routine will start to fall into place, and your baby will begin to understand what's happening on a daily basis. It's around this time that you have to also understand that while you decrease the amount of food your baby consumes at night, you have to compensate for that amount of food during the day because the calories that your baby needs to consume should still remain the same.

During the second and the third month, you will not be feeding your baby multiple times at night, and sometimes you will only have to wake up about two times to get your baby back to sleep. Besides feeding, you can also take up other methods of soothing to help your baby sleep; this might also be a great time to let your child learn how to self soothe. During the third to the fifth month, parents get really confused because they notice that their baby is up during the night more often. There is no need for you to worry if your baby is awake more often than you expect during the night because it is around this month when your child learns to play and gets excited at random things.

If you have chosen to give your baby the bottle instead of breast milk for any reason whatsoever, the fundamental feeding habits stay the same.

Cluster Feeding

A lot of parents tend to feed their baby more food several hours before the baby goes to bed so that the baby is able to digest their food better so that there are no problems while they are sleeping. If you are still breastfeeding your baby, then it might be a good idea to extract milk using a pump and give the baby the bottle a couple of times, choosing to breastfeed only when necessary. While you can still give your baby breast milk, constantly putting them to the breast will make them want only breast milk, and breaking the habit, later on, can get difficult. The reason you should pump milk at specific hours is that it then trains your body to produce less milk during the night, and this will increase your comfort level and help you sleep better.

Introducing the Bottle

If you have decided to reduce the number of breastmilk feeds that you give your baby, then you might also like to incorporate a formula; however, you might not want to do it all at once. Try to switch one meal to the formula, and gradually increase the number of formula meals you give your baby before they get used to formula completely. If you want to introduce formula, you may want to try after 6 months of breastfeeding because breastfeeding during the first 6 months is recommended; you shouldn't experiment with any other food sources for these first 6 months.

If you are having problems introducing the bottle to your baby, you are not alone. My daughter refused to take the bottle in, and every time I put the bottle into her mouth, she would start getting irritated and cry. Here are a few tips that I tried using with her, and I believe they will work for you too.

Slow Flow Nipple

Using a slow flow nipple to feed your baby is a preferred choice. When you are a parent, you are constantly tired. There is no denying that you would want to feed your baby as fast as possible so you can get a little extra time to relax; however, that's not a healthy habit. Some of the reasons why babies refuse the bottle is because it is very different than an actual nipple, and this is a difference they do not like. Breastfeeding allows the child to be in control of the amount of milk they want to take in, and that is what a slow flow nipple does. Most babies preferred this nipple to a faster one.

Holding the Baby in an Upright Position

When you hold your baby in a horizontal position, only the nipple has milk, and this enables your baby to drink milk slowly which makes them believe that they are being breastfed.

Encouraging

One of the best ways to get your baby to move on to a bottle is to gently brush the nipple on their lips and wait for them to open their mouth. Once they do, put the nipple into their mouth so they can begin drinking.

Bottle-Feeding Timing

When you start bottle feeding your baby, you have to be prepared to feed your baby for about 15 to 20 minutes. If you are feeding your baby at a faster pace, it's important that you slow down because it may take a toll on your baby's digestive system and your baby can develop colic. Babies need to breathe in between swallows, so give them time and don't force them to finish the milk fast.

Babies Can Smell

One of the reasons why babies refuse the bottle is because it does not smell like their mother. The reason I highly recommend substituting only one bottle of formula in between a breastmilk bottle is that it's easier to get your baby used to formula that way. Babies are a creature of habit and don't accept change that easily. Introducing one bottle of formula in between two breast milk feeds will make it easier for the baby to transition from breast milk to formula in comparison to abruptly changing from breast milk to formula.

Milk Supply

Most mothers are worried about their milk supply and whether or not their body will be able to produce enough milk when they need it and stop producing milk at certain times when they don't need it. Just like the sleep routine, your body also has a routine, and once you decide to pump out milk at a specific hour and you do not take out milk for the rest of the night, your body gradually reduces the amount of milk it produces at night. Similarly, when you start decreasing the amount of milk that you extract, your body starts to adjust and will only produce the amount of milk that your body needs to produce. The reason it is always recommended to make a slow transition from the breast to the bottle is that it gives you and your baby enough time to adapt to the change, thereby making it a smooth transition rather than one that is difficult to deal with.

Tips for Babies Who Refuse the Bottle

Kids understand the difference between breastmilk and bottle milk even if the bottle contains breastmilk. Most kids don't like to switch from the breast to the bottle. In such cases, you simply have to make sure that you lure them into using the bottle without forcing them to do so. Distraction is a great method to feed your baby out of the bottle. You can also try to imitate the breastfeeding position but give your baby the bottle instead.

Not the Breast

A child understands the difference between the feel of their mother's breast and an alien object. If it is difficult for you to get your baby to drink out of a bottle, you may want to ask your partner to help you with this. Let your partner step up and introduce the bottle even if this means you having to leave the room. This will help your baby detach from your breast and ensure that he transitions smoothly to the bottle.

Change In Environment

If there is a breastfeeding chair in your house or a particular spot that your baby associates with breastmilk, do not give the baby the bottle in that spot. Try taking your baby outside if necessary or hold your baby in a different position altogether to try to get them used to the bottle. I would take my baby girl to the window and hold her in my arms while feeding her through the bottle so she was constantly looking outside and was distracted. This worked like a charm every time, and she didn't even realize when she got hooked on to the bottle.

Try Out a New Technique

Sometimes your baby might not want to transition to the bottle, and that's where a pacifier comes in handy. When your baby is tired and playing in the crib, you can just try and put a pacifier in their mouth for them to get a little comforted. Then, give them the bottle after they have the pacifier in their mouth; this method may work out really well. This is because babies tend to drink milk before falling asleep. While nursing worked well for you initially, getting them to suck the bottle and sleep might be a little tougher. Using the pacifier and then introducing the bottle usually works well.

Don't Give Up

A lot of women tend to give up trying the bottle because the child was not getting used to it at all. You need to know that children take a while to get used to the bottle, and it could even take as long as a month sometimes. So you have to be patient and persistent in order for your baby to get used to a bottle. It will happen eventually, but if you give up, it's not going to happen at all.

Earlier, I listed how you can introduce healthy feeding habits to your baby. Let's take a closer look at the various ways to feed a child.

Child Chosen Feeds

Child chosen feeds, or CCF as I would like to refer to it, is a situation where you feed your baby when your child demands the food. This would mean waiting until your baby starts to cry or show signs of hunger before you feed them. While this may seem the most effective way to feed your child, it's actually not that effective. The reason why you shouldn't depend on your baby to know when they need to be fed is that children have erratic feeding habits, and if you depend on them, you will never be able to come up with a routine. Children are also always developing, and their thoughts and desires change with them. What may seem to be a hunger cry today may not necessarily be a cry for hunger a week from now. This means that you will constantly be guessing whether or not your baby needs to be fed, and this is something that will interfere with the routine and the sleep pattern as well as the general development pattern for your baby.

You are the primary caregiver, and it is up to you to decide when and how you should feed your baby rather than depending on your baby to show you signs of hunger. This doesn't mean that you completely eliminate this method. There could be times when your baby is a little hungry or you have given them a small meal which hasn't filled them up completely. If you notice that your baby is crying constantly, then feeding them is something that can help. CCF is something that is usually used for the first four months for an infant and then again once your kid starts talking and can tell you when she is hungry.

Time Chosen Feeds

As the name suggests, a time chosen feed is a feed that is given to a baby depending on what time of day it is. A lot of parents choose this method because they believe it is highly effective, and you will be able to time the feed of your child whenever necessary. While this seems like a great way to feed your baby, there is one problem. You begin to follow a timetable, and you will lead a rigid and very stressful life, making you depend on the clock for everything. While it is good to look at the clock every now and then, feeding your child based on time may not be as beneficial as you think it is because there are various external factors that could come in the way of this method of feeding, and it could create chaos in your life. If you want to lead a simple life without too much stress, then I do not recommend a time chosen feeding method because when you depend on the clock for everything you do, it will stress you out all the time. I tried this technique for a week and got so frustrated that I gave it up completely.

Parent Chosen Feeds

Here is a technique I really enjoy. PCF or parent chosen feeds is highly recommended for a number of reasons. It allows you to live a routine life without interfering with the various surprise elements that you may cross paths with on a regular basis. It will help you follow a routine that is not that rigid, and you can always make changes because it's flexible. If you noticed, I have always spoken about different feeding times, and the reason this is important is that although the feeding time is varied from time to time, it does not affect the routine in any way. Instead of deciding what time you feed your child, you need to plan how you will get to the feeding. Taking them to the park and then feeding them, irrespective of what time it is, works better for them rather than following a timetable. This is because children are curious and love looking around. The park has a number of things for them to get distracted by, and this can help you to feed them. You will be surprised to see how similar the time patterns are when you choose to feed them after following a routine, and this is a foolproof method because children are almost always hungry when you follow this plan. When they get used to a routine and their body starts to adapt to the various things that take place during the course of the day, it eventually helps them. This is also the easiest way to feed your child, and you don't have to wait for them to tell you or to check the clock to decide when to feed them.

Chapter 3:
Development Of Your Child

What Is Good For Your Baby

Solid Foods

Transitioning from breastfed to solids could be difficult for a baby if you try doing it all at once. However, if you gradually introduce your baby to solids a little at a time, not only will your baby manage to eat healthier, but he or she will also get all the nutrients that are required for a growing baby. While you should not consider starting a solid food diet for your baby for the first 6 months, once your baby crosses 6 months you can switch to foods other than breast milk.

If you are not able to nurse your baby, then the best thing for you to do would be to start off with formula. This will provide your baby with the necessary nutrients.

Once your baby reaches 6 months, you can start introducing solid foods into the diet. It is always healthier to introduce fresh food as opposed to packaged food because this is free of any chemicals and it provides your baby with ample nourishment. However, if you cannot provide your baby with fresh food because of a busy schedule, then you might want to check out some of the best brands you can purchase for your child. When choosing baby food brands, always look for the ones that are free of chemicals and pesticides as well as organic and natural.

When you have just started transitioning your baby from breast milk or formula milk to solid food, start off something that is semi-solid like a smoothie or a rice cereal that's in the form of a paste. Babies that are small don't have teeth as yet so the last thing you want is to give them something which is difficult for them to swallow and could cause them to choke. When you begin solid foods, make sure that you try small quantities first just so you know whether your baby can handle the food or whether your baby is allergic. Give your baby a lot of time to adjust to the food and once they have adjusted, never give your child something that he or she may not like. Fruits are a great way to begin solid food for your child but make sure that the fruits are always diluted properly and you don't give them too much of it because digestion could be difficult with certain fruits.

When your baby crosses 6 months, you can start giving your baby liquids in a feeder cup and you can also try giving food in larger quantities. Once you begin giving your baby solids, you will start to realize what your child enjoys eating and he/she does not. If you are matching vegetables and fruits together and there is a certain flavor that your baby doesn't like, try to cover it up with something your baby finds interesting or enjoys eating.

The larger the variety of food you introduce to your baby in the first two years, the more convenient it is for your baby to eat food without a fuss during the later stages of life. Rather than forcing your child to eat something they dislike, try to give them something they enjoy. This way, the encouragement is always there and they will clean up the plate without a fuss. Always try to include larger portions of vegetables and fruits in comparison to meat but also ensure that you include a fair amount of dairy in the diet of your choice.

Understanding What To Feed Your Baby

Switching from breast milk to solids is never an easy process and as a mother, you need to understand what works best for your baby. While some children enjoy eating fruits, there are others who absolutely hate it. If your child does not like something, you would be happier trying to feed them something else that provides them with the nutrients you want them to get without a fuss. There are also various ways you can camouflage fruits and vegetables to feed them to your babies without them realizing it. Milkshakes definitely work well with children and they manage to fill up on these effectively as well. It is also easier for children to start off with liquid-based solids before the transitioning stage so they are able to swallow more conveniently and you don't have to worry about them choking.

When you start off on solids, try to start feeding your baby small quantities of softer food so they understand how to chew the food properly before you try feeding them something that is hard.

You need to understand that children are used to swallowing when they are babies and it's going to take them a while to understand how to chew food before they swallow it. The softer the food, the lesser the chances of your child choking on it and the easier it is for them to learn how to chew food properly.

Don't Wait Too Long To Start Solids

Parents are always confused with regards to when they should start feeding their baby food other than breast milk. While some mothers choose to wait for up to 6 months, there are others that could go as long as 3 years without feeding the baby solid food. It is always preferred to start your baby off on solids after the first 6 months because this makes it convenient for the baby to understand the different kinds of food that they can eat and also how to react to the food. If you feel your baby is allergic to certain foods, then give them very small portions and see how they react to it.

Don't Give Your Baby Bland Food

The biggest mistake parents make is to believe they have to give the children food that has no flavor whatsoever because that's what helps the child digest. The truth is while you have to avoid spicy food, you may want to consider adding a little flavoring to the food to make it a little possible so that your child likes the taste. If you have to eat the same thing every day, it will annoy you and you would eventually dislike that meal, no matter how tasty it seems on the first day. It's the same with children. Try adding a bit of variety with their meals and experiment with different kinds of things you could give your baby. You need to understand that once you start feeding your baby solid food, you have to translation those habits into your child right up to the age of 5. Try to experiment with as many foods as possible and give your child a variety of foods they like. The stronger the eating habits as a baby, the more convenient it is for you to convince your child to eat a home-cooked healthy meal as opposed to ordering from outside and giving them fast food to eat.

Balance Out The Nutrients

For the first three years of your child's life, you have to focus on the brain and body development because at this stage the baby grows the fastest and absorbs as much information as they can. You need to give your baby plenty of iron, Omega 3, Vitamin D and Zinc in order for them to grow strong and intelligent. When choosing food items to give your baby, make sure that you ensure all of these are covered and keep changing the meals to ensure you cover every nutrient that is required during the day.

Don't Get Them Hooked On To Sweets

It's good to give your child a chocolate every now and then, but try not to make a habit out of it because children tend to crave sweets more often in comparison to others, and they would like to make it a main meal if they could. If you notice that your child craves a lot of sweets, try keeping the sweet things out of sight and try to include more fruits that are also sweet but healthy.

Know Went To Stop

Every baby is different and while some children have a large appetite, others may not necessarily eat so much. If you notice that your baby gets full fast and does not show any interest in eating anymore, do not force your child to eat. Instead, try to give them smaller meals more frequently so that their digestive system works well and they can manage to take in the food that they eat. If you try force-feeding your child, this food is going to waste because your child will throw up all the food which gets stored in the body as unnecessary fat. When you feed your child, you should avoid outside food that is unhealthy and only feed foods to your child that they can accept.

Tips To Help With Weaning Your Baby

The transition from the breast to the bottle or a feeding cup could take a while and if you want to make this transition as soon as possible, you need to give your child enough time and have a lot of patience. Children do not like a lot of change especially when it comes to their feeding habits. When you first introduce your baby to the bottle, try it with the best breast milk that has been pumped so they don't find a lot of change in the taste and learn how to adjust to it. If you try to feed your baby a different kind of food, it will be more difficult for your child to adjust in comparison to something that they are used to in a new environment. Once your child gets used to drinking breast milk out of a bottle, you might then want to slowly start introducing them to external foods a little at a time.

Slowly Reduce Breastfeeding

Once you introduce your baby to the bottle and you know for a fact that your child has become comfortable with the bottle, you can reduce the number of times you breastfeed your baby and replace it with the bottle.

Keep Your Baby Close

When you are trying to get your baby off the breast and onto a bottle or solid foods, always hold your baby close and comfort your baby while doing this.

Move Around

Moving around with your baby rather than sitting still can definitely work in your favor because kids tend to get distracted really fast and they like looking around. When they do that, slowly slip the bottle into their mouth and get them accustomed to it. The more you learn how to distract your child while feeding, the easier the feeding sessions will become.

Give Your Baby A Lot Of Attention

Breastfeeding doesn't just feed a child and keep them full, but it also gives them warmth and a feeling of security. When you take that away from them, you need to replace it by giving them more attention and always being close to them. While some children manage to get used to the bottle fast, there are others that take a long time so let your child get used to a new method of feeding on their own rather than forcing them to do it.

Cognitive Development

Cognitive development is one of the major reasons why some babies find it difficult to sleep even after they turn 4 months old. Your baby is usually aware around the four-month mark, and this level of awareness will keep increasing as each day passes. This usually causes a lot of sleep regression because your child is curious about everything around him, causing him to stay awake for as long as possible. The best thing to do in such a scenario is to create an environment around your child where she is not exposed to anything new. When they see the same things on a daily basis, their level of inquisitiveness will not be that high, and they will eventually soothe themselves to sleep.

There are various factors that could cause sleep problems with your baby, and you need to figure out what these factors are and how you can fix them. You also need to make note of certain points mentioned below in order to ensure that you correct your child's sleeping problems without causing too much disruption in their daily life. It is easy to overreact and do everything possible to ensure that your baby develops a healthy sleep habit; however, too many changes may cause other complications with your baby's health. Here are a few things that you need to keep in mind when you are trying to solve your child's sleep problems:

- Make changes to your child's routine to benefit them and not to benefit you. Your sole purpose should be to change your routine so that your baby benefits from it. You cannot force your child to go off to sleep at 7:00 p.m. just because you want to go out and party each and every night. You need to start being a responsible parent and develop a routine for your child that will help them become healthy.

- Avoid using stimulations to get your child to fall asleep. I know a few parents that try playing music or play the television for the child just so they can get tired and fall asleep. These stimulations do not work long term, and you need to find natural ways of getting your child to sleep on their own. From my experience, I learned that it is best to keep your child in a quiet and dark room. When you try to give your child the pacifier or the bottle to get them to sleep, they will start becoming dependent on this method.

- Avoid changing your child's sleeping position once they have fallen asleep. Always try to avoid getting a child to sleep on the couch or in your room and then shifting them to their room. If your child wakes up in a different place than where they fell asleep, they will usually feel startled and cry out for help.

- If you are adopting a waiting approach for your child, then you need to make sure that you do not start when they are too young. The waiting approach refers to holding back your urge to run towards the baby the minute you hear him or her cry. A parent should hold back for two minutes before they decide whether or not their baby needs attention. If a baby really needs you, they will continue crying beyond two minutes. If not, they will go back to sleep. Most children learn to fall asleep on their own once they reach the four-month mark. Forcing your child to sleep through the night is not advisable because most newborn babies do not sleep through the night. The sleep of a newborn is broken into various small maps, and you need to find out the sleeping pattern in order to solve any problems with your child's sleep.

- If your child has learned to fall asleep on their own but cannot go back to sleep if they wake up in the middle of the night, then you need to start focusing on that aspect rather than getting them to fall asleep at the start of the night.

- If you are a two-parent household, then you need to make sure that both of you share the responsibilities. It is very easy for partners to divide tasks in the household based on convenience; however, that is the wrong technique. You need to share responsibilities with one another because swapping duties with each other can make the task easier, and you will not feel stressed if you do not have to put your child to sleep every single night.

- Avoid waiting too long before you respond to your child's cries because some children tend to throw up or fall sick if the parents do not arrive soon.

- Under most circumstances, avoid using a sitter to put your child to sleep because your child will then get accustomed to the sitter being around.

Becoming a parent is an amazing experience, but it doesn't always go as planned. There are various problems that you may come across, and it's important that you keep yourself prepared for all of these so that you will be a better parent to your child and help them develop healthy habits. If you're worried about certain circumstances under which you got a baby, then here are a few ways to deal with these situations.

Premature Births

Most women are not prepared for premature birth, but the truth is that 1 out of 10 pregnant women will have a baby preterm. A premature baby is a baby that is born before the 37th week, and this means that the baby is a little more fragile and delicate as compared to a baby that was born full term.

Thankfully, there are modern methods that can help a preterm baby become healthy in no time, and if you had a preterm baby, there is nothing to worry about. Just make sure you listen to your doctor and follow their instructions correctly.

The pregnancy of a woman is divided into three terms. The first trimester, or the first 12 weeks of pregnancy, is when the fertilized egg starts growing slowly in the body. The second trimester, which starts after the 26th week, is the time when the baby starts to actually look like a human. The third trimester is when the baby begins to store water and fat in the body so that they can come outside. This is when the baby's heart, lungs, and skin develop and they learn how to breathe. If a baby is born at this time, then the baby is healthy and completely developed; however, babies that arrive before this will have a few problems and are considered to be preterm or premature babies.

Birth Between the 24th to the 26th Week

A baby born between the 24th to the 26th week is considered severely premature and requires close monitoring in order to become healthy again. Babies are usually born with underdeveloped lungs and could have serious health conditions, which is why they will need to stay on a ventilator until they develop and become healthy. Babies born in this time are also prone to more infections, which is why they need to be kept in a sanitized location. Some premature babies are also known to have bleeding in certain parts of the brain, which is why it is important to look after them closely and ensure they are taken care of in the NICU. A lot of parents are sure that their baby will not be able to lead a healthy life when they are born this early, but the truth is that with the right medication, many premature babies manage to develop into healthy infants.

Birth Between 27th to 29th Week

Babies born between the 27th to the 29th week are also considered premature and require serious care because these babies could be mildly or severely underdeveloped. Most premature babies have lung problems because of underdeveloped lungs, and this also increases the risk of infection. Bleeding in the brain is also a common problem for babies this small. Babies born between the 27th to 29th week need to be kept in the NICU for a few weeks to ensure they develop well and get healthy. These babies manage to survive when given proper care and nourishment. While a baby this small tends to sleep most of the time, some mothers are encouraged to spend time with their little one and begin nursing. This helps the mother and baby connect, and it also helps the baby to feel comforted outside the womb.

Birth Between 30th to 34th Week

Babies who are born after the 30th month are considered to be a little healthy and could have stronger lungs as compared to a baby born before the 30th week. While they are still considered to be premature and have the risk of bleeding in the brain, this risk is reduced considerably. Babies who are born after week 30 have stronger lungs, and the chances of survival are also higher. Babies that are born around week 30 have a survival chance of almost 90%.

Babies Born From 36th to 37th Week

A baby born between the 36th to 37th weeks is almost a full-term baby and is completely formed apart from a little weight issue. These babies have strong lungs, and the only major problem is that they will need to be treated regularly. No matter how premature your baby is, the right kind of treatment will help your baby become healthy. While a lot of parents fear that a premature baby will have health conditions all their life, the truth is that once your baby develops properly, they overcome prematurity. This is a temporary condition, and all you need to do is encourage your baby to catch up and grow healthy. Viral diseases are a big threat to premature babies. You need to take one step at a time to give them the right medication so that there are no health complications.

While some premature babies may need to be put on a feeding tube initially, they can then move on to feed on the breast or a bottle.

Babies are kept in an incubator so that they are kept warm and develop in a healthy way. It also helps the skin to grow in case a baby was born really early. A premature baby is very small, and it's difficult for these babies to handle the temperature outside of the mother's womb, which is why you may want to consider a warmer room even after your baby is brought home. Baby's lungs do not start functioning until the third week, so if your baby was born a little early, it is going to take your baby a while to learn to breathe properly. A little persistence and effort will pay off in the long run. A premature baby can turn out to be just as healthy as a baby born full-term, so don't lose hope! Miracles can happen.

Just like a full-term baby, a preterm baby is also known to develop a sleep pattern, so do not refrain from introducing a routine into your baby's life just because your baby was born preterm.

Multiple Births

Everyone gets excited when they are about to have a baby, and it is safe to say that with most cases that excitement doubles when they are about to have multiple babies. While multiple babies bring you multiple joys, there is also a lot of responsibility that you have to take on your shoulders. While triplets and quadruplets are not common, these days a number of women are giving birth to twins, so this is a possibility you shouldn't rule out. If you are carrying more than one baby in your stomach, you have to increase your responsibilities, and this includes understanding their feeding and sleeping habits. When there is more than one baby in your belly, the chance of premature delivery is also a little high, so make sure that you take good care of yourself. Since this book is dedicated to the sleeping habits of babies, let's talk about sleeping with multiple babies.

If you thought that you could follow a routine and give them food and get them in bed at the same time, this might not always work out as well as you would want it to because it's not necessarily the same for two children. While they may be twins or even triplets, their habits are a little different from each other, so you have to double up your responsibilities and create separate logs for every baby. What works for one of your children might not necessarily work for the other. You have to understand the routine of each child separately and plan accordingly.

When you have more than one baby, it can become difficult to cater to their eating requirements, and you may end up getting sleep deprived if you try to do this on your own. The best way to tackle multiple children is to start using a breast pump so that your partner can assist you with feeding the babies and form a routine effectively without taking a toll on your health. Sometimes when one baby wakes up, they automatically wake up the other one, and even if that baby isn't hungry, your baby will be crying and howling for attention. This is a great time to introduce self-soothing as well so that each baby learns to independently self soothe themselves rather than depend on each other. While you can keep them in the same room, it is highly recommended that you have separate bassinet cribs for multiple babies. Eventually, your multiple babies will learn not to wake each other up.

Traveling with Your Baby

One of the biggest fears of parents is about how the child is going to adjust to travels and if they have to enter a new time zone. Let's get one thing straight: your child has no clue about the hectic planning required to travel. They just enjoy being in the moment and even tend to enjoy the flight because it's comfortable and cozy. You don't have to worry about making a complete sleep routine for your baby when you are on vacation, but you can always follow the same things you did as the bedtime routine to help your baby go back to sleep whenever required. When you are traveling, it is important for you to keep your baby comfortable, so here are a few things you should try to do.

Keep your baby in cool, comfortable clothing so that they can move around easily rather than trying to make your baby look cute, especially for a long flight. Ideally, get your kid a pair of pajamas and a cozy t-shirt.

You can also carry a dark bin bag that you can stick on the window in case you want to create a dark atmosphere for your baby to sleep. If you are living in somebody's house, you can always ask them for dark curtains, and if you booked a hotel room, make sure to see if there is enough darkness for your baby to get comfortable.

When you are in the plane, make sure to take a seat on the aisle so you can stand up and down with your baby in order to put her to sleep. You can also invest in a portable crib that you can carry along with you so that your baby feels comforted and is sleeping in a similar place.

Your baby may take a while to adjust to a new location, so don't get stressed out about your baby not resting. Give your baby a little time, and he will adjust and be able to sleep well.

If you're visiting a new country and the time-zone is different from where you live, there's nothing to worry about. Your kid is less likely to be as jet-lagged as you are, and this means that it will be easier for your baby to sleep just as well even in a different time-zone without any problems.

Getting Used to the Routine

Kids may seem unpredictable, but in most cases, children get used to a routine and manage to sleep effectively while their mothers, on the other hand, struggle to fall asleep because they are worried and believe their babies want to wake up. There are a number of women who have told me they sleep with an eye open to ensure that they are always around when their baby needs them.

When you become a mother, you want to be a hands-on mother that is with your child all the time, which is not a bad thing to want. Whether your baby has come into your family naturally, through surrogacy or through adoption, the early months of having a baby are always sleepless, and parents tend to stay awake to make sure that the child is as comfortable as possible and they aren't sleeping through the child's quiet cries. You begin walking on eggshells, and you believe that you have to wait near the crib just in case your baby needs you. This eventually takes a toll on your life, and it does not work out in your favor because you tend to fall ill more often. You need to understand that after a few months, your baby is going to sleep for long hours, and the reason this routine is so helpful is that it's a foolproof method of ensuring your child isn't going to wake up before a certain time. This helps you relax, and you will manage to sleep more effectively. If you aren't able to do this, then discuss your problems with somebody and find a solution.

Sometimes mothers just need a little relaxation, and they will manage to sleep a lot better. I listen to some soothing music and read a good book before I head to bed. You can also enjoy a nice warm bath or go in for a massage. Spending some quality time with your partner is also a great way to relieve stress and resume your routine life all over again. Becoming a parent is a wonderful thing; the journey is more than fulfilling, but you will be able to enjoy it more when you are healthy and sleep better. Stick to my advice, and your baby will sleep well. Don't stress yourself out by staying awake. Turn off that night lamp and lay your head to rest!

Helping to Mould Your Baby's Brain

When your child is young, you need to make sure that you provide your baby's brain with enough stimuli to learn on its own. Babies learn from patterns at a very early age. The reason a child needs to do a certain task over and over again is that their attention span and their recalling capability is shorter. A 2-month-old baby will remember something for a couple of days, but a 3-month-old baby will remember it for approximately a week. However, if you go on repeating the same action over and over again, babies will tend to learn them over a period of time. By the time the baby reaches the 6-month mark, their visual cortex will have developed, and they will start associating certain actions with certain outcomes. Your baby will be used to social behavior in and around the house, and she will protest if she sees that you are changing certain routines. I tried to change my baby's sleep pattern over a period of time. It took me about two months to get a pattern in place, but I made it a gradual change rather than changing overnight. If you have been getting your baby to sleep at 6:00 p.m. every evening and you suddenly expect them to sleep at 7 p.m., it's not going to happen immediately. You need to move the clock forward by 5 minutes every night until they are accustomed to sleeping at 7:00 p.m.

Changing patterns takes a lot of patience, and you need to be smart about it. You think that your child does not notice a lot of things, but that is not the case. Children notice patterns and learn habits very quickly; this is the reason they are accustomed to certain sounds and sights at certain times. My child wanted her favorite bottle by her side when it was time for bed. When it was her sleep time, she made sure that she found the bottle from any corner of the house and brought it along to her bedside. That's when I realized that my baby was learning and was adjusting toward her sleep time.

Babies associate habits with certain actions and visuals. For example, if my parents came over, my daughter knew that it was only play time, and nothing else would interrupt her schedule. She also knew that when it got dark outside, it was no longer safe to go to the park, and she would not trust me to step out. These habits develop over a period of time, and you cannot force them onto your child. It's an automatic development of the brain, and these patterns and habits will come naturally to the child. One advantage of patterns with babies is they learn new patterns and forget the old ones very quickly. As I said, if you want your baby to learn something, you should try to get them accustomed to the new pattern by changing it gradually so that they forget what they were doing a week ago. If your baby has learned a bad habit, do not try to stop it overnight. Take advantage of the baby's inability to remember things from two or three days ago. This will help your child forget the bad habit and develop a new good one.

Try to associate good actions with sleep patterns for your baby. If you get your baby accustomed to sleeping near a noisy window or on your couch, there is a possibility that he will not be able to sleep in a very quiet environment or on a different surface. I always ensured that I put my baby down for a nap in her crib rather than on any other surface in the house. She very quickly developed the habit of falling asleep only when she was in a crib under a fan in her room. It helped me find a routine for her and developed the best sleep pattern for both of us.

The First Four Months

The first four months are very crucial for the baby and the parents. Most parents feel pressured into developing certain habits for the baby within these first four months. This is the reason they start force-feeding a baby at certain times during the day or forcing a baby to sleep at a time when they feel that they need to sleep. However, the first four months are crucial for you to learn what your baby wants to do and how he will naturally learn. You need to let the biological clock of the baby develop on its own. It takes a lot of time for a baby's nervous system to develop and for their body to fall into a routine.

In the first four months, the baby will be very scared and will try to adopt any routine that soothes him or her. You can use this to your advantage and start using soothing methods that will get the baby accustomed to certain sleep patterns. When you start soothing your baby at a time when she needs you the most, then the baby will start trusting you and will allow you to fine-tune their sleep pattern. Always try and meet your baby's needs within the first four months; however, make sure that you do not over-help. We have already spoken about unhelpful habits, and you need to stay clear of these habits in order to let your baby learn naturally. The baby's level of awareness will grow as they reach the four-month mark, and you need to be aware of this. Your child will start developing a regular routine, and most of their actions will be predictable by the time they reach this age. This is the reason I have broken down most of the chapters in this book into separate age groups. One speaks about the first four months, and the other is about babies that are five months and above.

Chapter 4:
Healthcare For Your Child

Pregnancy is tough and stressful, and your first pregnancy is usually going to be the most difficult because you don't really know what you should and shouldn't buy.

While it's essential for you to have a clear list of what's important, you should also understand unnecessary expenses and avoid them. I've discussed what needs to be avoided in the next chapter, and this one focuses on everything you need for your newborn baby. These are the kind of things you can add to your gift registry to cut down on your expenses and make sure you get the stuff you actually need.

Baby Diapers

You can never have enough diapers because babies need a lot of them and they go through at least five to seven changes a day and sometimes more, which means a pack of 50 diapers won't even last a week. There are some amazing baby infant diapers that you can invest in or add to your gift registry, so you are prepared when your baby poops. Make sure to select one that is designed for infant skin because an infant has very sensitive skin and using a diaper that is not designed for an infant could cause rash and infection.

Baby Wipes

Baby wipes are just as important as diapers because when you change your baby diapers you need something to clean up your baby and using cloth or cotton isn't recommended. If you are adding wipes to your gift registry, try registering for a bulk packet because these don't go bad for a long time and they will last you a couple of months. There are a number of baby wipes available so look for something that is soothing and designed for sensitive baby skin.

Diaper Rash Cream or Ointment

No matter how careful you are, your baby will end up with rashes on their bottom, and the best way to treat this rash or sore skin is to use a good quality baby rash cream or ointment. Always consult with your pediatrician to figure out which ointment or cream is good for your baby. You need to look for something that's not chemical based and has all organic natural materials, so it is safe on your baby's bottom.

Burp Cloth

It is highly recommended you invest in a ton of burp cloths because your baby is more likely to make a mess during the first three months and you should always be ready to clean up later on. This cloth usually comes in a bundle of either 3 or 6 so add about two or three bundles to your gift registry just to keep some extra handy.

Feeding Bottles and Storage Bags

A lot of women need to get back to work soon after they have had a baby and in such situations, you either need to pump milk out of the breast and store it in a bottle/bag or prepare formula for your baby. Irrespective of which route you take, you will need a lot of bottles and breast milk bags to store the milk. Try adding at least half a dozen bottles and bags to the list, so you have enough time to sterilize them before you use them.

Quick tip - Make sure you sterilize the bag and the bottle before you store milk in it because newborns are very sensitive, and the stomach cannot handle anything out of the ordinary.

Rubbing Alcohol and Cotton Swabs

Once you bring your baby back home from the hospital, you need to clean the umbilical cord. In order for you to do this, you have to use rubbing alcohol and cotton swabs. This is something not a lot of people will tell you about, and most mothers are not even prepared about what needs to be done in order for them to clean the umbilical cord regularly. Make sure to ask a midwife or the doctor to teach you the correct method of cleaning the cord, so you don't hurt your baby.

First Aid Kit

A first aid kit should be at the top of your priority list even before your baby is born. I didn't realize this until later when my husband panicked and ran out the door to the nearest pharmacy to get one.

Your first aid kit should have a nose sucker, thermometer and basic medications your doctor has recommended for your baby.

Nail Clippers

While we're on the subject of a first aid kit, I'd like to talk about the importance of nail clippers specifically designed for infants. Cutting the nails of a baby is so underrated, and parents usually believe they can use any nail clippers, but this is not the case. I didn't realize the importance of a nail clipper until I had scratch marks all over my breasts because it's my baby's long nails and my inability to cut them with an adult nail clipper. There are safe to use baby nail clippers available that you can safely cut your baby's nails with. I highly recommend getting one of these.

Baby Formula

If you plan on getting back to work in a few weeks post-delivery, you need to consider getting your baby used to the formula because you will not manage to pump out a lot of milk and store it in order to feed your baby throughout the day. While breastmilk is ideally recommended for the first six months, if you can't give your baby breastmilk you can always alternate between formula and breastmilk depending on how hectic your schedule is.

Pacifiers

Most babies need a pacifier to keep them calm and help them feel secure when they're not breastfeeding. If you plan on getting your baby a pacifier, look for soft pacifiers that won't hurt your babies' gums. Try investing in a couple of them so that you can keep sterilizing and cleaning them from time to time.

Breast Pump

I can't stress enough on how effective this pump was when I got back to work. While it is a personal choice, you can always try getting on manual one that doesn't cost so much and see whether it works well for you or not. The benefit of using a breast pump is that your baby is not dependent on you and you have a little freedom and time where you could just go relax and rejuvenate yourself.

Baby Lotion

Baby lotion is essential to ensure that the baby does not suffer from dry skin or any kind of rashes after having a bath. It is essential to make sure that your baby is comfortable once he or she has had a bath and al lotion will help soothe the skin from outside and keep it moist from within.

Washcloths

You need to have a few washcloths in hand when you have a baby around. It is important to know that your baby will drool most of the time and there will be a lot of wiping that you will need to do around the mouth and the chest area. It is best not using a towel because a towel may cause irritation to the baby's skin and this is where a washcloth will come very handy.

Baby Shampoo

You need to take care of your baby's hair from the first month itself. Apart from investing and lotions you also need to make sure you invest in the best baby shampoo that will help treat your baby's hair with care. There are a number of no-tear baby shampoo brands you can consider. You won't need to purchase a very big bottle because you need to use a very tiny drop each time you bathe your baby.

Baby Bathtub

Many people use adult bathtub to bathe their babies. It is important you purchase a baby bathtub, so your baby has his or her own space when they are having a bath. A baby bathtub is not slippery, and it is safe for babies to use. Adult bathtubs, on the other hand, can be slippery and if your baby has the habit of standing up while having a bath, this could cause accidents and unwanted injuries which could be avoided with the baby bathtub.

Crib Along with Mattress

Getting a crib for your baby is essential and you can also ensure that you get a crib that will match the decor of the baby room. While purchasing a crib, you also need to make sure you invest in a top-quality mattress that will keep your baby very comfortable. The reason you need to purchase a baby mattress is that you would not want a baby to sleep on anything that could irritate his or her skin.

Bed Linens

Newborns are extremely messy when it comes to pooping or even throwing up after eating. While it is not advisable to feed a baby in the crib, if you have to do that, you need to make sure you invest in a good set of bed linens. It is always good to invest in three or four sets of linens so that you can keep swapping them as and when the baby dirties one of them.

Blankets

Swaddling a newborn baby is essential, and this is why you need to purchase blankets that will help the baby feel extremely secure and warm. Newborn babies need to be wrapped tightly because they are used to being snug in the womb. This is where a swaddling blanket comes extremely handy. If your baby is not very comfortable with being swaddled, then you can leave one hand outside the blanket, and the baby will think that he or she is not wrapped.

Clothes for Your Baby

You will have to invest in various onesies and gowns that will make it easy for you to change the diaper for your baby. Most of the clothes for babies these days are available with the button at the bottom that will allow you to change the diaper very easily without having to take out the top. Clothes are available in various sizes but always make sure that you invest in something that would fit a 3-month-old because your baby would grow very fast, and there is no point in purchasing new clothes every month.

Socks

A newborn needs socks all the time. Although one may feel that they do not really need to cover their baby's feet in summer, it is important because your baby's skin is very sensitive, and you would not want to expose the skin to the elements. This is the reason you also need to purchase a hat that will come handy during the summer as well as the winter.

Car Seat

A car seat is the most important item that you need to purchase for your baby. You should always purchase a new car seat as opposed to purchasing a used car seat because the used car seat may not be able to withstand a crash. The installation of the car seat has to be done properly. Look for a car seat that has excellent safety ratings.

Stroller

It is important to have a stroller; however, you can always combine a stroller along with the car seat that you purchase. There are a number of brands that offer this combination; however, you need to check the safety aspect of the seat before you go ahead and get excited about the combo offer.

Diaper Bags

This is something that you will have to purchase irrespective of how old your baby is. When you move around with your baby outside the house, you will want to carry extra diapers along with creams as well as baby wipes. Always look for a diaper bag that has an insulated section that will help keep bottles cold or warm as per your food requirements.

Don't Fall for These Money Traps

Every parent looks to provide their baby with the best, and there's nothing wrong with this. However, you need to learn to draw a line between what's necessary for your baby and what is an unnecessary expense. There are going to be a lot of new parents who will come and advise you with regards to baby products that they believe are must-haves. Here are a few of these things I believe are a complete waste of money and should be avoided.

Baby Wipe Warmer

I never really understood the concept of a baby wipe warmer because you don't have to wipe your baby's bottom with a warm wipe since cold ones are always preferred. Warm wipes could cause a little irritation on your baby's skin, and unless you are storing your wipes in the freezer, you won't need this warmer. If it is really cold in the city you live in, just warm a little water and dip the wipe inside the water before using it on your baby. It's economical and makes a lot of sense.

Baby Seat

A baby seat is something you need to avoid, and while it has become a really popular item to have in a household, it is best avoided. It is dangerous forcing your baby to sit even before they are ready to walk, and this could cause a major accident. When your baby becomes ready to sit just use a normal chair!

Talcum Powder

Baby talcum powder has been really popular, and people are so used to patting the baby's bottoms with this powder every time they have a bath. However, this is best avoided because there have been reports of baby talcum powder being linked to ovarian cancer.

Baby Food Blender

A baby blender works just as effectively as your blender, and it does nothing different. You can blend your baby's food in your regular blender and investing in a baby blender makes no sense.

Expensive Swings and Rockers

Most new parents get frustrated when their baby does not sleep because they need to be held all the time. One of the things that most parents do is invest in expenses swings or rockers that they feel will put the baby to sleep. What these parents don't realize is the child will eventually start sleeping on their own, and the rocker will just be a waste of money lying in the corner of the room. As parents, you should take turns to hold the baby because this phase is not going to last long, and babies outgrow it very quickly.

Emergency Bottle and Formula

When you are not breastfeeding, it is always advisable to purchase formula because it will help provide nourishment to the baby. However, if you are breastfeeding and you do not have to feed anything else to the baby there is no point in purchasing formula just for the heck of it. Having formula around could even be a barrier to you breastfeeding your baby and this is the reason you need to keep it away for as long as possible when you are breastfeeding your baby.

Baby Shoes

These are a complete no-no. Your baby is not going to walk until he or she is about 7 to 8 months old. There is no point in purchasing shoes for a 1 month or 2-month-old baby because it is never going to be used. There are parents who spend hundreds of dollars on expensive branded shoes just because they want their baby to look good. Making such investments is of no use until your baby starts walking.

Baby Walkers

Let me make one thing straight - a walker will not teach your baby to walk. Most babies are able to figure out walking on their own. We should all remember that our parents learned to walk even when walkers were not even invented. Some babies learn to walk later than other babies; however, this should not be a cause for concern. Forcing your baby to walk with the assistance of a walker is definitely not recommended.

Hooded Towels

Babies need towels however, they do not need towels that come with a hood. Babies grow at a very fast pace in the first year and purchasing a towel with the tiny little hood will be of no use in a couple of weeks.

Pregnancy is a long and beautiful journey that has its ups and downs. While you can try to figure out a few hacks to help you through your journey, you also need to remind yourself that every individual is different and what works well for someone else may not work as effectively for you. Take time to figure out your rhythm, and you'll get better with each day.

The journey of parenting begins from conception, and it's a role you need to live up to, every day of your life. While you'll enjoy it for the most part, for the times you don't - just take a deep breath and start over! It's not about perfection, but about enjoying parenthood and making the most of it.

Uncovering the Facts About SIDS

One of the biggest fears for most parents is SIDS. SIDS is sudden infant death syndrome, and this is usually related to the sleep environment and the sleeping position of the child. It most commonly occurs in children that are less than 1 year old. Most medical investigations have not been able to explain this sudden death phenomenon. In most of the cases, the child suddenly stops breathing, and their heart stops beating. 90% of SIDS cases happen within the first 6 months, and there are a few things you can do to avoid this risk. The risk of SIDS is usually noticed in children that are premature or of low birth weight. Smoking by the mother during pregnancy and no prenatal care are also a couple of factors that affect SIDS.

One of the major risks for SIDS is when the child sleeps in a facedown position. There are some doctors that will ask you to make a child sleep in this position if they know that your child is not at risk for SIDS. However, if your doctor has not advised you to do so, then you need to always make your child sleep on his or her back. If you feel that lying on the back for prolonged hours can cause discomfort to your child, you can also try to move her to her side but never facedown. Some pediatricians and also a few parents hear that if they make their baby sleep on their back, they might choke if they vomit in their sleep, but this has never been the problem. SIDS is a bigger problem than choking during sleep, so you need to make sure that your child sleeps on his back.

Another problem that may occur by making a child sleep on their back is the back of the head may become flat. This is because the skull is still forming and can take any shape if exposed to pressure for prolonged hours. To avoid this, try turning your baby's head from side to side regularly. You can also try to turn the crib away from the light and towards the light at certain times; this will make your baby turn his or her head automatically away from the light. As compared to the flattening of the back of the head, SIDS is a lot more dangerous. Your baby's head will correct itself, but a baby affected by SIDS will not recover.

By the age of 6 months, the baby will be able to turn from his back to his stomach, but at this stage, the risk of SIDS would be lower. You should also ensure that your child does not sleep on a surface that is not specifically designed for infants, for example, a water bed, a soft sofa, quilt, pillow or sheepskin. When a baby sleeps on soft surfaces or is tucked under loose bedding, there is always the risk of suffocation. Suffocation also occurs when certain parents choose co-sleeping over independent sleeping. When you are co-sleeping with your child and one of the parents is overweight, there is a risk of entrapment and of overlying where the parent may roll over the infant. As absurd as this may sound, there have been cases of entrapment that have been reported in the past. You can never be too sure when it comes to your baby's sleeping position, and you need to do everything possible to ensure that there is no chance of suffocation or entrapment.

Another major cause of SIDS can be cigarette smoking in and around the house. You should also avoid overheating your child. You need to dress your child according to the temperature in the house as well as the temperature outside. Overlapping your child in bedding and clothes will cause overheating, and this can also result in suffocation.

Chapter 5:
Understanding Sleep Patterns

The first year of the baby will bring about a lot of challenges, and you need to know what to expect in each of the months.

The First Four Months

The first four months are extremely crucial, and you need to set a proper routine for your child's bedtime. There are a number of parents that encourage self-soothing, while others opt for parent help. During the first four months, your child may not sleep through the night, but they will eventually learn to sleep for long hours if you establish good sleep patterns and develop the best sleep environment in the house. If you want your child to sleep at 7:00 p.m., you cannot play loud music in the house or watch television at a very loud volume. You need to get your habits in place in order to establish good habits for your child. You also need to find the right balance between soothing and self-soothing. Too much of either one can backfire on you. A newborn child usually has a lot of fear; this is why you will see most parents swaying and rocking their child. While this can initially help your child, they have to learn self-soothing in order to fall asleep. Overdependence on soothing by parents will cause sleep hindrances as your child grows older.

5 Months to a Year

Once a baby crosses the five-month mark, you will see a transformation in your child's mood. Some babies tend to laugh all the time, while others continue babbling from the 5th month onwards. You will start seeing the excitement in the baby's eyes, and he will start becoming aware of what's around them. This is because the frontal cortex of the brain is starting to develop. This will help the baby self soothe, which is why you will see a lot of babies moving back and forth in order to calm themselves or even sucking on their hand or thumb. Some grab their feet and put them into their mouth, while others slowly hum to themselves. All this is behavior that is triggered by the brain, and it helps a baby to self soothe when the parents are not around. Bedtime will no longer be a struggle because the baby will have found a rhythm and a fixed schedule. You no longer have to tiptoe around the baby because your child will get into REM sleep almost immediately. Avoid the use of a pacifier as much as possible because there have been cases where babies do choke on the pacifier while they are in deep sleep. Your ability to balance between soothing and self-soothing in the first four months will pay off from the fifth month onwards.

Sleep Timeline

There are a few things that you need to expect throughout the baby's life cycle. When the baby is a newborn, their sleep cycle will be very irregular; your baby will keep going to sleep and waking up depending on the sleep cycle that you are trying to maintain for her. An irregular sleep pattern can be difficult to handle; however, since a baby is so young, you can mold the sleep pattern based on what you think is best for the baby. When the baby turns about 8 weeks old, he will start sleeping more frequently but in an unpredictable pattern. The baby will have one long stretch of sleep at night which will last anywhere between 4 to 8 hours and several daytime naps that will have no specific length. Once a baby grows old and reaches the 3-month mark, the baby will start sleeping more at night and stay awake during the daytime. Although the sleep pattern will still be fairly irregular, the lengths will be more or less predictable depending on what you are trying to imbibe in the baby. When the baby crosses the 5 to 6-month mark, they will be able to sleep for longer stretches at night. The stretches could last anywhere between 10 to 12 hours, and this would be a very regular cycle from this point on.

Swaddling

Swaddling is an important part of parental care, and you need to do it correctly. Here are a few points to remember when you are swaddling your baby:

- When laying a baby down to swaddle, you should always lay them on their back.

- Use fabrics that are breathable, and make sure that you do not overdress the baby at any point in time.

- You need to keep the room temperature cool in order to keep the baby comfortable.

- After you have swaddled your baby, make sure that there are no loose blankets around the sleeping surface.

- You need to stop swaddling your baby once she starts rolling over. This can increase the risk of suffocation for the baby.

- If your baby has started kicking a lot, then make sure that you stop swaddling the baby immediately. You can start using pajamas or blanket sleepers in case the baby kicks a lot at night.

- Make sure that you leave sufficient room for the baby's legs to move around and bend because this will help the hips to develop. When the baby cannot move his or her legs around, the hip joints will become stiff and cause a lot of damage to the soft cartilages. Make sure you keep the upper body wrapped very snugly.

- When swaddling the baby's arms, make sure that the elbows are bent and you keep the arms in a folded position on the chest. This is the position they took in the womb, and this helps with developing the joints and keeping the baby calm as well. Your baby will try to suck his thumb, as this is their natural instinct. You need to give them the opportunity to do that even when they are swaddled.

- When your baby has outgrown the swaddling phase, you can choose to go cold turkey or you can start gradually. You can try transitioning with one or two arms out of the swaddle for a few nights and eventually take away the swaddle altogether.

Sleeping Practices

Now that we've spoken about the various ways that you can swaddle your baby and regulate his sleep pattern, I also want to share with you some sleeping practices that I believe are safe for your baby.

- The initial few months are crucial for your baby, so make sure that you share your room, except your bed, with your baby. The initial risk of SIDS can be lowered considerably if the baby shares the same room as his parents.

- I cannot stress this enough: you need to make sure that you put your baby on their back while putting them to sleep.

- When laying a child down to sleep, always ensure that you put them on a firm surface. Avoid using a mattress that is old or has been used a lot. Some parents even try using car seats to make the baby sleep; however, that is not recommended at all.

- Avoid placing any loose bedding or any kind of soft objects around the bed. These objects can increase the risk of suffocation and could be really harmful. All you need is a blanket along with a pillow and a simple sheet.

- Avoid placing a hat on the baby while they are sleeping.

- You can use a pacifier while putting a baby to sleep; however, once the pacifier falls out, there is no need for you to reinsert it.

- Always ensure that the room is not too hot so that your baby stays as comfortable as possible.

- Do not keep the room too still, and have a small fan that will keep a little air moving around the room.

- Always avoid smoke exposure to the baby and keep alcohol and drugs away for as long as possible - forever if possible.

- Immunize the baby as per the recommendations of a doctor.

Stepping Up Towards Responsibility to Achieve Stability

Finding the right balance between assisted sleeping and independent sleeping is important for every parent. In order to build a healthy relationship, parents need to make sure they do not overprotect their child or provide too much help when not required. Babies need to deal with certain problems on their own, and while this may sound harsh, it will only make sure that your baby gets stronger and more independent as she continues to grow.

Let us take a classic example: almost every child is afraid of the dark, and when you stay in the room with your child because he is too afraid to close his eyes, you are unnecessarily being too helpful. Children need to learn to cope with the darkness on their own, and this can only be done with the right approach. This chapter will show you how I balanced the approach towards my children and helped them grow and get over their fears.

Helicopter Parenting

Don't get me wrong - all children need a lot of love and parental touch. The sense of touch and warmth of a mother's womb helps a child build trust and keeps them comfortable while they learn new things around them. You will see this with primates as well as other animals; children tend to stay too close to their mother while they are exploring the world. This attachment theory helps researchers around the world understand the development of the child through the different stages they go through.

However, there are a number of parents that misunderstand this attachment and end up codling their child at every possible juncture. You will see a lot of parents encouraging their children to stick to them even when it is not required. In such a scenario, the children will not learn on their own and will not be ready for the challenges that the world will throw at them later on in life. Independence is important, and you need to encourage this independence from an early age. Parents tend to swoop in anytime there is a problem, and this is what is called helicopter parenting. Helicopter parenting is something that usually happens at night, and this is when the attachment gets taken very seriously. You will see a lot of parents exhausted because they follow this helicopter parenting method. I also suffered from this when I had my first child; however, I learned that finding the right balance will take care of my sleep problems and will help my child develop as well.

Parents who adopt the attachment approach of parenting will often hamper the child's ability to learn on their own, which will even hamper the child's independence. Most parents do not realize what the attachment approach will do. Let us take a classic example of a child playing with a shape sorter. Children love the shape sorter game, and it helps develop the brain to make logical decisions. While the child may learn to eventually sort the shapes and put them in the right slots, you cannot afford to get impatient with the child and help them place the shapes in the right slots. If you help your child place one shape in the slot, the child will automatically hand over the next shape to you and expect you to do it for him. This is the same thing that happens when it comes to sleep. If you help your child sleep for one particular night, there is a very good chance that they will look for you the next night as well. This is when they start to get dependent and cranky. Always remember one simple rule: if your child is able to do something on their own, then do not take away the chance for them to learn to do it. Struggling is a part of life, but when you try to take away the struggle from your child's life completely, they will never learn. You need to know when to give your baby space and when to respond to their cries for help. You need to find the right balance between over-helping and under-helping. This will help your child to learn and respond to you in the right manner.

When it comes to sleep, you need to make sure that you do not adopt any extreme methods in order to put your child to sleep. Some parents try to adopt the under-helping method where they put the child to sleep, shut the door and try not to respond to the child at all. This is one of the meanest methods that you can adopt in order to put your child to sleep. You should also stay away from over-helping, like getting into the crib with your child or rocking them to sleep. Finding the right balance between these two methods will help your child learn naturally and sleep better.

Helping Older Children

By the time your child has crossed the 6-month mark, there is a very good possibility that she has begun to sleep well. While you will still be responsive to older children, you need to make sure that you allow your child the space to feel secure and confident. You need to have clear expectations with a child and make sure that they understand their responsibilities with regard to sleep.

The First Steps Towards Parenting

Sleep is extremely important for the health and development of a person. You can compensate in terms of food and exercise, but you will realize just how important sleep is to your body. A baby's brain has already developed the need for good sleep from the time they were in the womb. While a number of people may think that it is difficult to develop a sleep pattern for a baby, let me tell you that it is not that difficult. Imagine the amount of time you will have to yourself if your baby is sleeping on time. Getting a full night's sleep is no longer a dream, and I will help you make it a reality. You need to have a plan in mind if you want your child to develop a stable sleep pattern. If your child develops a healthy sleep pattern, it will help them learn and remember things much better. This was probably one thing you didn't know, and even I wasn't aware of it when my first child was born. My daughter was having difficulty sleeping, and when I consulted the doctor, he informed me that her brain's prefrontal cortex would not develop properly if she continued missing sleep. You are probably wondering what the prefrontal cortex is. It's just a part of the brain that helps with our decision making. This certainly scared me because I did not want my daughter falling behind with her grades once she began school. Most studies have shown that kids that sleep less than 10 hours a day do not score as well in their cognitive tests.

Another plausible explanation for your child crying all the time is because he or she could be hungry. If you are lost as to why your child is hungry all the time, it is because of what happened in your womb. When your child was inside your womb, you offered him or her everything that was needed. Your child would consume all the food and then go off to sleep. These were the only two activities your child did inside your womb. Now that they are outside, they feel a weird sensation in their stomach called hunger. They do not understand what hunger is, and all they know is that if they cry, they can make the sensation go away. The only way a baby can communicate is by crying, and the initial few days will be spent crying in order to get attention and to try and subside the hunger in the stomach.

Baby's Sleep Dilemma

If you are facing a problem with the sleep patterns of your child, then your child could have a problem. This problem could arise because of a disorder - emotional or physical - or it could just be a normal reaction to the things happening around him. Sometimes you will be able to detect that your baby has a problem, while on other occasions you may not realize it. Some of the most common problems that parents face are for example difficulty to get their baby to fall asleep, their baby waking up in the middle of the night and not being able to go back to sleep without her parents being there, their baby waking up very late in the morning, their baby sleeping very late or very early in the evening or their baby being extra sleepy during the day. For some parents, it is easy to identify problems because their children suffer from sleepwalking, bedwetting or in some cases even sleep terrors.

However, some parents do not recognize their child's sleep disorder, and they often call them lazy for being sleepy during the day. Some parents notice that their children are snoring but do not realize that snoring can also be a sign of a breathing disorder; if this is not treated properly, it can start interfering with your baby's sleep. If you do not identify that a child has a sleeping problem, it will eventually start affecting their behavior and their learning abilities. Every child has a different number of hours they must sleep to feel well-rested, and you cannot determine that number for them. All you need to do is make sure that your child is active when he or she is awake and does not wake up at odd hours every single night.

Your Baby's Slumber Routines

A person usually alternates between REM sleep and non-REM sleep. The amount of REM sleep that one gets depends on their age and also various external factors. As your child grows older, their REM sleep time will keep increasing and their non-REM sleep time will keep decreasing. When a newborn child sleeps, he immediately enters the REM sleep stage. When she reaches her third month, she will enter the non-REM stage first and then move on to the REM stage. This is the pattern that will continue throughout your baby's life. This stage 4 level of sleep is what most adults slip into after the non-REM sleep stage. Stage 4 is a very deep level of sleep that most adults would have developed by adolescence. A child also reaches stage 4 of REM sleep on a daily basis for a couple of hours. When you wake your child, if he is in stage 4 of REM sleep, he may not recall being woken up the next morning. Let's look at an example: when your child falls asleep in the car and you carry him back to the house in your arms, change his clothes and get him to sleep without him even realizing, this is stage 4 of REM sleep. Sleep terrors and sleepwalking usually occur during this stage.

How Much Does One Need to Sleep?

As mentioned above, there is no specific number of hours your child needs to sleep on a daily basis. However, there are certain sleep needs that you need to take care of depending on the age of the child. Let's look at the age groups and the approximate number of hours that they need to sleep on a daily basis.

- Newborns: Newborns that fall between the age of 0 to 2 months usually need about 12 to 18 hours of sleep on a daily basis.

- Infants: Infants that fall between the age of 3 to 11 months require about 14 to 15 hours of sleep on a daily basis.

- Toddlers: Toddlers that fall between the age of 1 to 3 years require about 12 to 14 hours of sleep on a daily basis.

- Preschoolers: Preschoolers are children that fall between the age of 3 and 5 years, and they require about 11 to 13 hours of sleep daily.

- School-age: School-age is usually between 5 and 10 years, and children of this age need to sleep for about 10 to 11 hours daily.

- Preteens and teens: This is the age group between 10 and 17, and children in this age group need to sleep between 8 to 9.5 hours daily.

- Adults: Anyone above the age of 18 needs to sleep for a minimum of 7 to 9 hours on a daily basis.

You should know that these numbers do not necessarily indicate a fixed sleeping pattern. These are ideal scenarios that will help a person get proper rest and feel rejuvenated the next day.

Getting Your Baby into the Right Sleeping Habit

Figuring out how to get your baby to sleep is one of the biggest scientific experiments a parent can undergo. Although there haven't been any tests to see how to train a baby to sleep in the best possible manner, a parent can definitely try out certain techniques that can help the infants rest better and encourage their babies to form healthy patterns. The biological need of a child is very different than that of an adult, and that's why they cannot sleep for longer hours without waking up in need of something. You need to figure out a way to deal with the biological needs of your child.

As surprising as it may sound, parents usually influence the sleep patterns of a child from as early as the age of 5 months. You can't just begin trying to influence your child to sleep better once they have reached the five-month mark, which is why you have to start as soon as you bring them home.

Once you understand the basic factors that determine the sleep patterns of a baby, it will become easy for you to form a pattern for your child to follow, which will encourage your baby to sleep peacefully thus waking up happy and more active. A sleep-deprived baby is dull, but a well-rested baby develops better and is more active and happy.

Co-Sleeping

Many parents encourage co-sleeping which is allowing a baby to sleep in bed with the parents. This is a highly controversial topic because while some parents believe that they should always keep their babies close to them and coddle them while sleeping, there are others who are completely against this practice.

Children tend to adapt to the kind of lifestyle that you provide to them. This means that if you place the crib in the next room, they will fall asleep just as effectively as they would if they were lying beside you in bed. There is no psychological evidence to prove that co-sleeping is beneficial for your baby or that putting them to sleep alone develops insecurities. Some parents are just more confident allowing their babies to sleep independently, while others still have the fright of something going wrong which is why they want their baby in close proximity to them. As a parent, you should be free to try out what you believe works best for your baby which is why you should choose whether you want your baby to sleep in bed with you or in a crib to learn to sleep independently. I personally believe it's better to leave your baby in a crib because there is a risk of hurting your baby when she is in the same bed as you. It also creates an uncomfortable situation because parents tend to try and sleep with the least amount of movement so that they do not get too close to their baby. While co-sleeping may seem like a perfectly healthy alternative to leaving your baby to sleep independently, you need to remember that patterns are something that form in your child when they are just a few months old, and independence is definitely something you will want your child to exhibit from a young age.

Let's not forget that privacy is important to everyone, and children have just as much right to privacy as an adult does. If you form a co-sleeping habit for your child when they are small, they will more than likely want to stay in bed with you even when they grow up, and this will create uncomfortable living situations for the entire family. When a child gets comfortable sleeping in bed with you, they will not want to move out of the bed even when they are a few years old. This will also become a problem if there is a new child in the house because your older child will not want to move out of the bed and will still want to sleep by your side.

When children form a sleep pattern, they tend to follow it more rigidly than parents do. If you need to stay up past your child's bedtime to get certain work done, it will be difficult for your child to sleep with the distraction around them. When they have their own independence, you can always tuck your baby in and make sure they follow the pattern regularly.

Most children who sleep independently tend to have a sound sleep 99% of the time from when the lights are turned off to the time they wake up in the morning. If anything, these children will be awake for a maximum of 10 minutes during the night just to get into a comfortable position to fall asleep again. This simply means that it doesn't really matter whether there is somebody with the child or not. They will manage to sleep effectively as long as you train them well.

Instead of worrying about co-sleeping and making sure that you are there with your baby in the night, it is more important for you to spend time with them when they are awake. They don't really care about you at night while they are asleep because they aren't conscious. What matters to them is who is there with them to nurture them and care for them when they are awake. For your child to be healthy and sleep properly, you have to create an environment that makes your child confident and feel secure to be able to sleep independently. Most monsters that children believe in only exist because of the stories that are created by their parents. This is something you should try to avoid doing when you are raising your child, and you should make them strong and independent individuals who are able to face the toughest scenarios. It is the responsibility of a parent to take away the anxious feelings of a child rather than build on them.

Unless you have space issues, co-sleeping isn't something you should consider doing because it takes away the independence of a child and destroys the sleep pattern. Even if you have to have your child sleep in the same room as you, it is always recommended they have their own sleeping space such as a crib or a bassinet so that they learn to sleep independently without having to have somebody by their side all the time.

If you are uncomfortable with the idea of your baby sleeping alone, then you should try to train your brain to understand that your baby is going to be fine sleeping in another room. Do not let your fear influence your decision.

If this is something you cannot do, then you should give yourself some time to try transitioning away from co-sleeping to give your child the independence they need. While this is going to be a lot more difficult for you, you should try to get rid of co-sleeping as soon as possible. If you cannot stop co-sleeping, they will not be able to stop co-sleeping either, which will be embarrassing for them. They will not be able to sleep alone and will never be able to go for sleepovers with their friends. Developmental issues begin with really small problems, and co-sleeping, in my opinion, is one of them.

Advantages of Co-Sleeping

- Always in close proximity to your child
- Immediate parental support
- Comfortable nursing solutions
- Spend more time with your baby

Disadvantages of Co-Sleeping

- Increased risk of SIDS
- Poor sleep for parents
- Parents tend to get separated (sleeping in separate rooms)
- Sleep cycles do not coincide
- Parents have to sleep at the same time that the children go to sleep
- Sleep problems start developing
- No privacy

There is no denying that the advantages of co-sleeping are very limited in comparison to the disadvantages. This is why you should learn how to train your baby to sleep independently right from the beginning.

Healthy Bedtime Routine

Performing a healthy bedtime routine is something that will benefit your child from a young age. Babies who learn to follow a routine manage to self soothe themselves and fall asleep much easier. This also helps them to get more sleep during the night, thereby keeping them healthy and more active. Children have certain wants and needs that need to be fulfilled at a particular time, and once you figure it out, you will be able to follow the routine much better.

Children are very quick to learn a routine, and once they start following those routines, they do not like change. The hardest thing for a parent is to stick to a routine, especially when they are used to living an erratic lifestyle that involves absolutely no fixed time to go to bed or wake up. Once you are a parent, the most important thing for you will be to stick to a routine because that's when you will be able to form a sleep pattern for your child that will help them self soothe and figure out when they actually need you.

A routine is something that you should incorporate on a regular basis so that your baby knows what will follow next and automatically tune their habits to do those things on a daily basis.

Your bedtime routine should be no longer than about 45 minutes to an hour, and everything mentioned on the list should be completed within that timespan so that your baby understands and anticipates what's going to happen next. If you try to extend this routine to a longer time, your kid will not be able to adjust to it so easily. When you put your baby in bed, make sure to say the same thing to your baby every night so they know that they have to go to sleep the minute you leave the room. This could be something like 'Goodnight,' 'Sleep tight' or 'I love you.' Remember to keep this consistent as it will become a part of your baby's routine.

Feeding Time Versus Sleep

One of the most important things to remember when planning a bedtime routine is that feeding shouldn't be the last part of your baby's bedtime routine. This could create uncomfortable sleeping habits. Babies may not be able to digest the food if they are put to bed immediately after feeding, and this means it could take them longer to fall asleep. Listening to soothing songs works well because it helps the baby to self soothe as they go to bed. Some children like to be swayed from side to side while others like to be placed on the shoulder before they fall asleep. Figuring out which way works well for your child is definitely going to be part of the routine. Babies tend to wake up when you go down to place them in their crib, but gently patting them on their chest will help them to go back to sleep just as effectively.

The Final Steps Before Bedtime

When you take the final steps into the bedroom, it could feel like you are literally putting down a time bomb, and your heart will always beat very quickly, hoping that your baby doesn't wake up again. If you follow the bedtime routine effectively, there is only a slim chance your baby will wake up crying once you put them down. The one thing you should remember while placing your baby down on the bed is to try and keep the light as dim as possible and ensure that the room is quiet and cozy.

Here are some interesting ways you can initiate self-soothing for your baby:

Put Your Baby in Bed When Awake

This may sound really scary, but when you put your baby down in their crib when they are awake, they will not find anything wrong with it.

As opposed to yelling and crying to be carried, they will start reasoning with the fact that they need to sleep in their bed. This happens mainly because of the habit you've formed of placing your baby in bed to rest. Babies tend to pick up on routines, and when placed in bed when they are still awake and tired, they understand it's time to rest.

Increase the Time Frame Between Feeding and Sleeping

Try disassociating feeding just before your baby sleeps. Try getting your baby out of the routine eventually.

Learn to Ignore Certain Sounds

If your baby starts whining, grunting or babbling, you may want to stop yourself from going and scooping up your baby instantly because these sounds can be the start of self-soothing.

Use a Time Barrier

If your baby is awake and is crying, wait for a minute before you head to your baby because sometimes babies can go back to sleep after crying for about a minute. However, if they cry for longer, do not ignore those cries and head straight to your baby.

Independence

As much as you want to spend every waking minute of your time with your baby, you need to give your baby a little space so that you train them to be independent and you can go back to living your routine life. While in this stage, you want nothing more than to spend your entire life with your little one, but you should realize that it's not possible. It will be more difficult for you to separate from your baby when you spend so much time around them.

Tummy Time

When your baby tries to sleep on their stomach, it means she is trying to get comfortable with sleeping positions and is learning to self soothe more effectively.

Naps

It is difficult to understand the nap time of a baby initially, and this is why the first 4 months are quite confusing. Babies can sleep for as little as 5 minutes or as long as 3 hours. If your baby always sleeps at a particular time, then it's easy to understand that they will rest for 1 to 3 hours. That's the kind of time that you can give yourself to relax. Whether you want to take a nap, get a long warm shower, eat without having to hurry your meal or just admire your baby, do it. Babies tend to sleep a lot during the day, especially if they could not get enough rest at night. Even if your baby is asleep during the day, try to bring in a little sunlight during the day so that they subconsciously understand the difference between daytime sleeping and nighttime sleeping.

During the first four months, your baby is not going to be capable of sleeping for long hours, and this is the time self-soothing should definitely be introduced because it helps to encourage your baby to sleep better.

Catnaps

Short naps or catnaps are most common from the first to the fourth month, and this means the baby will be awake for a long time and sleep for short spans. This is usually because your baby will need to be fed multiple times or even changed. They tend to frighten themselves or startle themselves more often, and this causes them to wake up almost instantly. Once your baby has learned how to self soothe, it becomes easier for them to sleep a little longer. You will start to notice that they tend to sleep for 3 hours or so more comfortably.

What Causes Your Baby to Wake Up?

In case you were not aware already, you should know that all babies wake up multiple times through the night. Irrespective of whether the child is a light sleeper or a sound sleeper, there will be various stages when the child will wake up throughout the night. You will notice this in adults as well. There are certain stages throughout the night when an adult would wake up to roll to the other side or just adjust their blanket. These are the stages when you are not really awake, and you may not even recollect doing this the next morning. Your baby would also partially wake up multiple times through the night to do the very same things that you do - adjust their blanket, rollover or even grab their favorite soft toys (if you are comfortable placing them in their crib).

Some of these babies soothe themselves back to sleep, while others cry out for help from their parents. Most babies will forget what caused them to sleep in the first place, and they do not have the ability to self soothe themselves yet; this is the reason they look for assistance from their parents. If you have assisted your baby in sleeping by rocking her in your arms or by feeding her, then your baby will look for these actions when they partially wake up in the middle of the night. The same would happen to an adult as well. If an adult falls asleep in a comfortable environment and wakes up in a completely new environment in the middle of the night, they would find it very difficult to go back to sleep. This is the same thing that happens with your baby.

You need to start finding the right balance between sleep associations so that your child does not find it difficult to go back to sleep when they partially wake up in the middle of the night. Sleep associations are actions that can soothe your baby and put them back to sleep immediately. This could be the rocking motion of the parent, listening to their favorite nursery rhymes or even listening to a bedtime story. When you start getting them used to such sleep associations, they will want you to recreate the exact action when they wake up in the middle of the night. If you are not able to recreate them, they will never go back to sleep. Let us understand each of these associations and whether or not they will prove useful to your baby.

Useful Sleep Associations

- Soft blankets or stuffed animals
- Babies rocking their body back and forth on their own
- Sounds of nature or complete silence
- Sucking the thumb or the fingers
- Getting comfortable in their favorite sleep position
- Babbling to themselves in the crib while falling asleep

Sleep Associations that May Prove Unhelpful

- Rocking your baby or bouncing them to sleep
- Breastfeeding or bottle-feeding your baby to sleep
- Using a vibrating chair, a swing or any other similar devices
- Playing music to get them to sleep
- Using pacifiers that cannot be re-inserted by the baby
- Taking short car trips or stroller rides through the neighborhood

Sleep Wave

Sleep wave is a technique that can help you find the right balance between being too helpful and staying away from your child when needed. Let's assume your baby girl is crying in her bedroom. There are various questions that will pop up in your head around this time. Is she fine? How long do I let her be alone? Should I go right now and calm her down? You need to remember that if you don't go in at all, your child will start wondering what happened to you and why you have suddenly disappeared. This will take away the trust factor, and your child will stop calling out to you for help. But if you go in too soon, your child will get dependent on you to soothe her back to sleep. This is where the sleep wave can help you. It will let you respond and also let your child know that you are not there to soothe her back to sleep. With the sleep wave technique, you need to pass the soothing baton to your child.

Babies usually find very sweet ways of falling asleep. Some babies lean their legs against the side of the cradle while others roll over to their belly. There are some babies that also nuzzle their blankets. Each baby has a unique ability that will help them go to sleep on their own. You need to find out what technique your baby adopts, and you will only be able to do that when you give your baby the space to employ the technique. In the sleep wave method, the parent needs to take on the role of a wave and rhythmically visit the baby's room. By rhythmically, I mean repetitively moving in and out. This can be a swift movement that will last about fifteen seconds. Your baby will notice this pattern every time he cries, and this will become a habit. When you move in and out of the room like a wave without immersing yourself in the soothing process, your baby will respond positively and start practicing self-soothing. This is one of the best ways for your child to go off to sleep, and the sleep wave method can be a great way to encourage self-soothing in your children.

Conclusion

Experiencing Parenthood is a beautiful emotion that can't be penned down in words. While the journey is exciting, there are a number of hurdles that new parents come across. It is important for parents to understand how to look after their baby in the most effective way and the right kind of food to help a baby develop and grow. Caring for your newborn and making sure you give your baby the best is vital. This detailed book not only helps you to learn how to nurture and nourish the needs of your child in the most effective manner, but it also helps you to understand the importance of caring and understanding your baby as well as what works for you and your baby. If you approach parenting the right way, you will be able to provide the best for your child and it will benefit you too. You will also learn how to transcend from being an experimental parent to an hands-on one with regards to all the needs of your baby.

Parenting is an ongoing process, and each day is a stepping stone toward learning something new. When I first became a mother, I had a ton of questions in my head. One of them was: 'Will I ever get to sleep?' There is no denying that the sleep habits of a baby are very different from those of an adult, and unless you get used to the sleeping patterns, you will end up getting frustrated and annoyed by your baby waking up every couple of hours.

Lack of sleep is something almost all new parents need to learn to cope with because your baby has different needs. While you need to be as sensitive as possible toward your baby's needs, you will end up with sleepless nights, and that could get annoying.

The reason I came up with this book is that I want all new parents to understand that it's normal for you to struggle to get your baby to sleep for a couple of hours before they wake up again. Sleeplessness is part of parenting, and if you cannot accept that, you'll constantly struggle to try different things to get your baby to sleep.

While it's easier said than done, there are definitely techniques that can help your baby sleep a little longer and also help them to understand the importance of balancing sleep time versus wake time more effectively.

If you want to get this done, you have to learn how to provide them with their necessities in a timely manner so you and your baby stay healthy and happy. I put together this book after a lot of experimenting and guidance from some of the best professionals I could find. I thought labor was the most difficult part of having a baby; the truth is the sleepless nights turned out to be way worse than I imagined!

Let me tell you one thing: once your maternal instincts kick in, you will not want to sleep unless you know your baby is resting. This means even if you look like a zombie and you have erratic mood swings, you won't be able to rest.

It's important for a baby's caregivers to stay healthy and well-rested if you want to bring up the child in a healthy and positive way. I wrote this book because I've heard a number of parents complain about struggling and not being able to sleep, and I believe them because I was once one of them.

Reading this book will not only help you to figure out an effective way to help your baby, but it will help you to train your baby in a way that will help them when they grow up as well. I understand that there are a lot of parents out there living a modernized life, nothing like the traditional marriage. Whether you are single, in a relationship, married, straight or gay, this book is still applicable to you. From learning how to tackle your first breastfeeding experience, to understanding what your baby needs and helping you with all the problems associated newborn care, I hope this book has covered up all your needs and gives you everything you're looking for!

Do let us know how this book helped you by leaving a review. This will encourage eager parents to make the right purchase, also I get motivation whenever I hear someone who gets value from what I created.

Happy Parenting!

In case you have not already done, remember to download this free tool. Click on this link to download this free tool

https://bit.ly/2FAGaqX

Note: If you have purchased the paperback format then you need to write this link on your browser search bar. This tool is a useful resource to understand the development of the language and communication of children. It is also a checklist on language and listening skills that will provide you with effective tips. All in all, it is a fundamental tool that will help you become an expert on parenting!!

Made in the USA
Columbia, SC
22 September 2019